i

VISION Paperbacks, a division of
Satin Publications Ltd
20 Queen Anne Street
London W1M 0AY
email enquiries to sheenadewan@compuserve.com

Cover design ©1999 Nickolai Globe
Layout by Justine Hounam
Printed in the UK by Bath Press Ltd.

FAME
The Psychology of Stardom

The Authors:

After initially training and working as a journalist, **Andy Evans** attended the Royal Academy of Music and then worked as a jazz musician until his mid thirties. Having become aware of the many problems performing artists faced in their careers, he trained as a psychologist and co-founded Arts Psychology Consultants in London in 1989, a practice staffed by psychologists who had similar backgrounds in the arts. Since then he has seen hundreds of private clients in the arts and media, specialising in career issues, creativity and performance psychology. He frequently broadcasts and advises the press on issues around celebrity, and is a consultant to the English National Opera and the Dancers Resettlement Trust. His published work includes 'Across the Cevennes' 1964, 'The Secrets of Musical Confidence' 1994, and a chpater in 'The Musician's Hand' 1998.

Dr Glenn D. Wilson is a Reader in Personality at the University of London Institute of Psychiatry and one of Britain's best known psychologists. An expert on individual differences, sexual behaviour, and psychology applied to the performing arts. He has published more than 150 scientific articles and 25 books, including The Psychology of Conservatism, The Experimental Study of Freudian Theories (with HJ Eysenek), Love and Instinct, The Great Sex Divide, and Psychology for Performing Artists: Butterflies and Bouquets. He makes frequent radio and TV appearances and has lectured widely abroad, having been a guest of the Italian Cultural Association, and a visiting professor at California State University, Los Angeles, San Francisco State University, Stanford University, the University of Nevada, Reno and Sierra Nevada College. Apart from being a professional psychologist, Dr Wilson trained as an opera singer at the Guildhall School of Music and Drama in London and still undertakes professional engagements as an actor, singer and director.

CONTENTS

FOREWORD

Fame is a growing phenomenon. The rise of mass media in the 20th century means that we live our lives more and more vicariously and we get to know celebrities almost as well as our intimate circle. In a world flooded with familiar media faces we also find that the distinction between the truly famous and the mere celebrity has widened over the years. Hollywood producers offer ever increasing millions to the small handful of stars capable of 'carrying' a movie in their own right. And because of the sheer numbers of well-known people before the public, being 'hot' is the key to succeeding. When magazines want to run an interview or advertisers seek someone to endorse their product they want only the 'hottest' names - the top footballer, the funniest comedian, the most popular DJ, or the most credible professor. The result is enormous salary differentials, large sums paid by the media to people with sensational stories to tell, and a desire to climb the ladder of fame that has increased exponentially.

Only by understanding this can we understand why people go to such extraordinary lengths to get media coverage. They streak in public, bare their souls on chat shows, get married and divorced for publicity, and produce 'art' that is calculated to be as obscene and shocking as possible. If all else fails, some people who feel ignored will shoot an established celebrity or massacre schoolchildren in their playground. At least that way they get noticed and their life stories appear in the media. Incidents like these are not unique to the modern age but they are certainly more and more common.

As psychologists whose work deals with the media and the performing arts we are often asked to comment on famous people, their personality characteristics, how they got to be where they are, and the problems they so often seem to have in coping with their celebrity, whether sudden or long-standing. The ethics of our profession prevent us from diagnosing or otherwise "analysing" the mental health of named, living individuals. We would not speculate, for example, as to whether Diana, Princess of Wales was suffering from "borderline" or "histrionic" personality disorder (questions which were often put by newspapers before her death, but curiously never after). It is, however, possible to make a number of general points based on the scientific literature and on actual clinical experience that help reveal the issues faced by people in the public eye, and to give advice on problems they encounter such as stage fright or burnout. This is what we have attempted to do in this book.

Inevitably, we have used illustrative examples that relate to known individuals, but in doing so we have tried not to go beyond material that is already in the public domain and hence could not damage those individuals further. To mention Bill Clinton's adultery at this stage, for example, should be no more hurtful than referring to the Kennedys' involvement with Marilyn Monroe. Therefore, readers seeking revelations and scandals about today's celebrities will be disappointed. But for those seeking to understand the phenomena of stardom and celebrity in general terms, we hope that the pages that follow will be entertaining and fruitful.

Andy Evans and Glenn Wilson
London, May 1999

WHENCE FAME?

"I don't want to achieve immortality through my work. I want to achieve it through not dying" Woody Allen

It is clear to all who have spent any time thinking about the phenomenon of fame that it is something which has changed considerably throughout the ages. This process of change has reflected changes in society. In times of constant war the famous were either heroes who saved their peoples, or spiritual leaders who offered salvation of the soul. In times of discovery the famous were explorers and inventors. In the media age the famous are simply those who are most familiar to the worldwide media audience. We have gone from being famous for deeds good or bad to being famous simply for being well-known. The cynic would claim that what was considered the 'moral' emptiness of fame in previous ages now applies even to the emptiness of its definition: "The celebrity is a person who is well-known for his well-knownness" (Boorstin, 1962).

It could be claimed that fame has undergone a democratisation process, where in the words of artist Andy Warhol anyone can be 'famous for 15 minutes'. Yet democratisation is the key difference between the Old Testament, a religion based on a hierarchical power base of a people with land and kings, and the New Testament, the religion of a downtrodden people where the meek had as much right to the earth as the strong. Through this democratisation a person possessed only of the clothes he stood up in, the power of his speech and his 'miraculous' personality could become arguably the most important person in history.

What has perhaps disappeared from fame is this miraculous dimension that was so much the trademark of the ancient pre-scientific civilisations. With it has disappeared much of the awesome quality of fear induced by such heavenly commotions as thunder, lightning, eclipses, floods, earthquakes and plagues. Aside from the miraculous there remain essential similarities between the first ages of mankind, where the difference between the 'mortal' and the 'immortal' was a cornerstone of society and its constructs, and our modern world of today, whose 'stars' mark the division between the world of the ordinary and that of the extraordinary.

Fame

THE GODS AND THE STARS

If we take a journey back to the earliest civilisations of Man we already find there a primitive, but highly functional 'star system' in the shapes of the early gods and goddesses. They may have been far removed from the Hollywood award ceremonies, but weren't these the 'Oscars' of their time? They had specific gifts, were the 'best in their categories', and had a timeless quality that qualified them for the Hall of Fame. Like a Marilyn Monroe or a John Wayne they personified what they did in a unique way. They all lived together in a world that was half real and half fantasy: Mount Olympus, though grounded on the earth was believed to "penetrate with its lofty summit into heaven itself". (Smith, 1867) So when Hollywood became a latter-day Olympus, the 'Home of the gods' became the home of the stars of the 'A' list.

'The Warrior' (Ares) was typified by mythical figures like Hercules, whose marriage with the youthful Hebe was an early version of 'Tarzan and Jane'. Historically, the 'warrior' figure was personified by actual kings and conquerors like Alexander, Genghis Khan and Napoleon (all the subjects of many films). Later it was symbolised by sports heroes such as the boxers Joe Louis, Muhammad Ali, and Mike Tyson, and film stars such as Sylvester Stallone ('Rambo') and Arnold Schwarzenegger ('Terminator'). The 'warrior-with-brains' figure has appeared in many forms from The Lone Ranger, Batman, and Superman to the 'gentleman warriors' like Robin Hood, James Bond and Sherlock Holmes. The female versions are Athena – strength with brains – symbolised by such as Lucy Lawless (Xena, Warrior Princess) and Artemis, the hunter and lover of nature, whose contemporary form of the physically fit and ecologically aware female was symbolised by Princess Diana (ironically also the Roman name for Artemis).

Zeus, the 'top god' was like Moses and Ghandi, who were known as the 'fathers of their people' to distinguish them from mere kings: "He is called the father of gods and men, the most high and powerful of the immortals, whom all others obey. He is the supreme ruler, who with his counsel manages everything, the founder of kingly power and of law and order. According to his own choice he assigns good or evil to mortals and fate itself is subordinate to him." (Smith, 1867) At the other end of the scale his brother Hades, who was given the underworld to rule, was like such contemporary villains as Fu Manchu, Moriarty or Goldfinger. In the later Roman Empire, deification became commonplace for a succession of emperors whose achievements ranged from the honourable to – in the case of Nero and Caligula – the unspeakably corrupt or perverse. In an era of repression and violence, cruelty was elevated to entertainment and part of the political function of the 'god' was to evoke fear. Whole populations were subjected to the ritual of placating the gods with animal or even human sacrifices.

The masculine embodiment of beauty, Apollo, is symbolised by Hollywood leading males like Brando, Newman and Redford, while the younger Adonis corresponds to stars like Leonardo di Caprio. The female beauty, Aphrodite, is represented by women such as Bardot, Deneuve and Monroe. The cute flirt – Eros – would be played out by Meg Ryan or the charming but diminutive Dudley Moore, and by child actors like Mickey Rooney and Shirley Temple. We assume these days that gods such as Apollo and Artemis were 'sex symbols', but for the Greeks those famous twins represented chastity and self control, unlike Aphrodite and Zeus who bedded their way around Olympus. In true soap opera style Aphrodite's son Eros was not even sure if his father was Zeus, Hermes or Ares. For an entertaining account of the Gods and their Star equivalents, see Leigh-Kile (1999).

One notion of archetypes, including those of physical beauty, is that they are timeless definitions: "One function a star serves is to fix a type of beauty, to help a physical type identify itself." (Jarvie, 1970) Such types of beauty become strong enough to defy fashion, or to rotate as fashion rotates between such poles as fat and thin, meek and aggressive, girlie and tomboy, earthy and imaginative. The human form of the archetype is necessary to make the image credible and to arouse our human instincts – in the case of sex symbols the desire to have sex with them in a 'fantasy' way. If anyone doubts this, let them read the threads on the Internet movie newsgroups, where you will find 'most bonkable contemporary actress', 'most psychotic bonkable actress', 'most bonkable actress in old movies' to name but a few.

MORTALITY AND IMMORTALITY

The analogy with the Greek and Roman gods and goddesses continues with the idea of mortality and immortality. They were human in that they could appear on earth, but immortal in that they could live forever – again, the essential qualities of the stars of today. They moved among mortals and so had a human comprehensibility, as in the

Fame

Christian ideology of God working 'through' man or his son being someone who 'walked among us'. In the same way, the stars of today 'walk
among us' – arousing a similar type of awe and disbelief when they do.
Like the stars of today the early gods and goddesses sometimes resort-
ed to disguises. You could be in awe if you met them, as with powerful
beasts, lions, serpents and other mythical animals. They also had the
same shock value – in the case of the primitive legends they could literally turn you into stone, as the stars of today symbolically make you
'freeze'.

The old gods and goddesses, however, lived in a pre-scientific age
and it would be hard today to replicate their 'mythical' magic powers
that went beyond the human. They could, in the eyes of man, do mira-
cles, or transform one person, animal or thing into another. We can
and do simulate these powers in the cinema, with extra-terrestrial
storylines and morphing effects. We also have magicians like David
Copperfield and Yuri Geller who promote the idea that they have
'supernatural' powers. And doctors and scientists have not reached
the limit of what they can do with humans – cryogenics, cloning and
research into mortality itself may be just a start. Perhaps we are return-
ing to the original ideas of immortality after all, but at the end of the
20th century our 'stars' are still distinctly human in body, however
much their images or screen roles may transcend this.

The point about the gods, goddesses and immortals is not so much
that they lived or didn't live. It is surely that in the minds of the people
they were immortal. You could call it projection or you could call it
wish fulfilment: both psychoanalytical terms. As humans we have a
basic need to find something that refutes our primal fear – that of disappearing forever into an unknown void. We also have a need to confront
our primal insecurity and doubt – even if death is certain we still do
not know when, where and how. What we try to create, therefore, is
some illusion of permanence. The desire for permanence drives people
to carve their name on trees and rocks, just like the handprints on
Hollywood Boulevard. We need to have an impact on life – to leave
something behind us when we go. We erect monuments to ourselves
and hold ceremonies to remember those who died in war. We simply
do not want people to die, and even less so those we regard as great
or unique. We do not want to forget such people, even though forgetting and change is central to life. As Pope put it, they are "damn'd to

everlasting fame" (An Essay on Man).

As a race, we 'leave behind' our genes, and thus a blueprint of our unique qualities. But these genes are mixed and diluted by half for every generation. Without cloning, there will never be another Elvis or another Charlie Parker (nicknamed 'Bird' for his soaring sax solos). Their uniqueness is remembered through look-alikes and sound-alikes, and graffiti saying 'Bird Lives!'. This simulated continuation of one life's uniqueness is close to what Richard Dawkins in 'The Selfish Gene' calls "memes" – examples of cultural genetics which prolong characteristics of our culture. (Dawkins, 1976)

If our lives are ultimately about confronting and surpassing death, then this implies the idea of beating time itself. This means beating the ageing process, and all aspects of mortality. It means being, like the stars in 'They Died Too Young' (ed. Hall), eternally youthful, transfixed as if in amber, like the youthful James Dean or the incomparable Ayrton Senna. Even where lives are not cut short by death, it means being frozen in a moment of glory, like Olympic athletes at their peak. It adds to child actors and even teenagers that poignancy of existing in a soon-to-be-changed ephemeral time bubble, which Hollywood has exploited throughout its whole history. It is no accident that California is the plastic surgery capital of the world.

FAME'S BRIEF CANDLE

'Forever' only applies to symbols – stars as actual people lose their lustre, and this is nowhere more true than in the case of sex symbols. If we take the case of Brigitte Bardot, it is only the charismatic icon transfixed in time that remains the 'star', not the ageing person now preoccupied with animal welfare. The 'image' of the star may be based on a small part of that star's actual life, or even the most famous roles with which the image was established. Because sexual allure is biologically linked to fertility, particularly in the case of women, very few (with the exception of Cher, Goldie Hawn or Susan Sarandon) are given the opportunity to carry a movie after 50. Their male counterparts remain stars at the age of sixty (Sean Connery, Clint Eastwood).

What defines a star? Amount of money made in one year? Fame for a given role? Eligibility to be called upon for new roles? Longevity in being selected for roles? Because star status requires the actor to be 'hot', the fame of actors usually enjoys a heyday and then fades. Cary

Fame

Grant puts it this way – "In Hollywood we have what I call 'A Streetcar Named Aspire'. The thing about this particular streetcar is that it is only so big, and there are only so many seats on it. When I got on, for example, Warren Baxter had to get off. When Tyrone Power got on, Ronald Coleman had to get off. Of course some got off more slowly than others, and some even ran around to the front and got on again as character actors (Adolphe Menjou). And a few never got off like Clark Gable and Gary Cooper."(Leigh-Kile 1999)

'THE BEST' AND 'THE MOST' OF HUMAN QUALITIES
"The history of the world is but the biography of great men." Thomas Carlyle

If the concept of transcendence of the mortal is central to the godlike quality of fame, then so is the transcendence of expected mortal qualities. These can be humane qualities like heroism or caring or inhumane qualities as with serial murderers or assassins. It can often be a question of who does something first – whether a Columbus or Neil Armstrong, or a scientist like Marconi or Pasteur. It can be a matter of doing something best – whether immeasurably in art like Bach or Shakespeare, or measurably in sport like Carl Lewis or Babe Ruth. It can be a whole raft of other things from the important to the trivial, as documented in the Guinness Book of Records. And on the sporting level, as on the trivial level, 'the best' may change very rapidly, so that with the passing of a year the record books may be substantially different. This is partly because you can run faster and faster and eat more and more boiled eggs for a bet, but only one person can be first to walk on the Moon. The 'firsts' often outrank the 'bests', because their achievements are absolute, and because they act as the milestones of human history.

Our human psychology needs markers to remember the vast array of information surrounding us in space and time. We find it easier to memorise letter groups like DNA or PVC than the expanded versions of what they stand for. As with mnemonics, the letters provide little prompts from which we can recover much richer material. Actors use keywords to help them learn large speeches – usually the beginnings of sentences or paragraphs that serve as landmarks to orient them. Similarly, our cultural history includes key individuals or 'markers', such as Einstein or Picasso to help us understand what science or art can achieve, and also to act as reference points. Even a ten year old child can say to another 'Who do you think you are – Einstein?'

As we need markers, we also need to place information in categories and rank order – something we use psychology itself for. We want to know the year's best actors – The Oscars – and then the 100 best movie stars of all time – the Empire list. Then the 100 richest people in Britain, the greatest people of the millennium and so on. We rank by wealth, popularity, sexual attractiveness, most records sold, most number one hits. Even within fame there are endless rankings – we seem obsessed with the concepts of good, better, best.

GOOD SOCIAL FAME
The word Fame originally meant 'good reputation', hence the association of the great and the glorious. There are the Mother Theresas who were famous for good human qualities, and to those go the award of Sainthood. There were those who worked hard for good causes, and to those go the Public Honours for good service. There were the titles and gifts of land given by kings to their loyal followers. In a symbolic way such titles are imitated in the showbiz world by calling Elvis 'the King' or by self styled titles such as Duke Ellington or Count Basie. But in the arena of war, public honours and a share in any profits were more luck than judgement – you enjoyed them if your side won. Exceptionally, fame in defeat went to those like Napoleon or Alexander who transcended what was imagined to be militarily possible.

We again come across quick ways of encoding information with our heroes, and here we use one of the tricks of professional 'memory men' – that of association of one thing with a striking or unusual image. Napoleon is paired with distinctive hat, Alexander with elephants, Hitler with moustache and military salute. We remember British kings in the same way – Canute and his tide, Alfred and his cakes, Harold and his arrow in the eye, Henry VIII and his wives. Sometimes the mnemonic becomes better known than the person, as with the heel of Achilles.

At times what is memorable is a pairing of two people with features that interrelate dynamically, as Anthony and Cleopatra symbolise love or Laurel and Hardy symbolise comedy. It also helps anyone to have a 'trademark' like Churchill's cigar, a memorable mutual dynamic (as 'endless pursuit' characterises Tom and Jerry in the cartoon world) or even a few memorable lines to say. These can symbolise achievement, as when Caesar uttered 'I came, I saw, I conquered', or they can be amusingly anecdotal, as when Stanley said 'Dr. Livingstone, I presume'. Either way, they certainly preserve fame through history.

MOVEMENTS AND THEIR LEADERS

Life can be confusing, perplexing and fraught with difficulties. In group psychology, if you put a number of people in a difficult situation needing a solution, they will within a short period of time choose a leader who seems to have more vision or ability, or whose opinions seem more 'right' than the others. Leaders often emerge from an environment of discontent – spiritual as with Jesus and Mohammed, or political as with Chairman Mao. Their solutions became literature, and their books – The New Testament, the Koran, the Little Red Book – became the 'answers' that their people sought at the time. At least in the case of the first two these have also stood the test of time.

Other leaders like Caesar simply wrote their military memoirs, while military theorists like Machiavelli became more important for their opinions than their actions. In the world of art, movements also showed a new way of perception, whether Impressionism, Cubism, or any other 'ism'. Such leaders and their movements helped whole peoples to think and see in new ways. And while their books and paintings are beautiful in their own right, they are not necessarily elitist – a Monet or a Van Gogh is easily appreciated by young and old of all levels of society. Other leaders, from Plato and Aristotle onwards, helped us think in new and dynamic ways. They also had schools of followers, sometimes made up of the élite and sometimes of the masses. Freud discovered how famous he was when he travelled to America by boat and found his cabin boy reading one of his books – it had already become a best seller.

With ideologies that have mass appeal there needs to be a basic foundation in the human emotions. The four main emotions dealt with in 'client centred' counselling work are assumed to be happiness, sadness, anger and fear. For a movement to have maximum impact, it would have to replace primary fear – that of oppression, injury or death – with something preferable. It could be replaced by anger in revolutionary movements such as the French revolution or the Black Panthers, which created heroes out of Robespierre and Malcolm X. Or it could be replaced by happiness in the shape of eternal life and the love of God. Anger is a solution where there is a reasonable expectation of change to an unjust system. Happiness on another level is a solution where the fundamentals – such as death or poverty – cannot be changed, or where one has to 'turn the other cheek'. Anger may be sublimated into qualities like the endurance of suffering, or it may be changed into forgiveness and acceptance which offer the relief of letting it go. In all cases enormous fame can be given to those like Jesus and Mohammed who offer ordinary humans a perceived escape from their fundamental fears and problems.

Built into any movement is the fellowship, solidarity and collective power of a large group with a common purpose. This is equally true of fan behaviour, where the fun of being in a group of fans may be as important as the worship of its idol. Fan behaviour also exhibits the same ranking principle as other groups. Those close to the leader get more personal access, and other tokens of closeness are used, such as autographs, signed memorabilia and possessions like clothes and musical instruments. As with holy relics, the act of touching is important, since it denotes actual rather than symbolic contact.

INFAMY AND SENSATIONAL FAME

"To murder thousands gives eternal fame." Edward Young

When Ghengis Khan was voted 'Man of the Millennium' in a US poll it was certainly not for being a nice guy: it was for wreaking a trail of destruction over Asia and Europe the like of which has rarely been seen. This was the man who justified himself by saying "I destroyed because people had done wrong – if they hadn't why would God have sent me to punish them?" His posthumous fame might have been for his military genius, but in his lifetime it was based simply on fear of his awesome machine of destruction. This power over life and death takes us back to the gods of history and to the most basic and primitive fear of their wrath. The same awe about humans who take the power over another's death into their hands – the murderers and assassins of history – results in the fame of serial murderers like Jack the Ripper and of destroyers of great men, like John Wilkes Booth.

Even history's murderers have been glorified in legend. There are the brigands, outlaws and gangsters – Jesse James, Bonnie and Clyde, Dick Turpin, Al Capone – and their seafaring cousins Bluebeard and

Fame

Surcouf. The awe in this case comes from the fact that they existed outside the law, again transcending the mortal laws by which others live. Some became sensational by being outside the 'normal curve' of the population in physical terms. People like the Elephant Man were exploited through no fault of their own, and were a stark contrast to the persecutors of history and those like the Borgias, who redefined parameters like cruelty.

While the persecutors reigned in the military arena, a different race of those who dared reigned in the moral arena. The moral transgressors were often women who used their attractiveness for power, like Mata Hari. Then there were the women who simply fell into mutually attractive relationships with famous people, like Nell Gwynne, Lillie Langtry, Mrs Simpson, or Monica Lewinsky, causing ripples throughout history and redefining the parameters of marriage and monarchy. There is a fine line between the moral transgressor and the free thinker – essentially they are the same in that they question the mores and morals of society. Sometimes it is only the hindsight of history that can distinguish one from the other. Since the outcome of the French Revolution was considered positive, its leaders would be considered freedom fighters rather than terrorists, in the same way that the leaders of the Russian Revolution would be classed as free thinkers rather than moral transgressors. Sometimes even historical judgements are morally perplexing – how did Henry VIII keep his crown and his successor Edward VIII lose his, when the issue in both cases was one of divorce?

TEMPORARY FAME AND CELEBRITY

The crucial parameters of fame are place and time. Many people are well-known within small or medium size groups – from village to town to nation. Few are famous around the entire world – while some popular music and sports like tennis and golf are universal, much popular music and also many sports like cricket or baseball are quite insular. And while there are attempts at 'world news' by the likes of CNN and the BBC, there is usually a substantial political spin, both in choice and in the presentation of what is considered relevant.

Many are famous for a short time, but forgotten quickly. Those that are 'news' such as the mother of the latest sextuplets, septuplets or octuplets may get a few months of media interest. Their fame is often sensational – whatever tugs at human emotions and fears. The same limited lifespan of celebrity applies to politicians and also to almost all those who, like sports people and dancers, are by definition only interesting at their physical peak. The arts are slightly different in that painters, authors, film stars and musicians leave tangible records behind them, so their minor celebrity status may endure as long as there is surviving hardware or software of their talent, or as long as there is enough public interest to keep them in print.

Public interest and the insatiable appetite for celebrities is behind another phenomenon of fame – the paradox of being 'Famous for being Famous'. Celebrities like Elizabeth Taylor, ZaZa Gabor and John Wayne remained famous long after their screen roles thinned out. They became, in their own lifetimes, archetypes symbolising the oft-married woman or the craggy faced male hero whose charisma and sexual attraction seems to beat the ravages of time. What are they good at? Simply being themselves, with a lot of help from good PR. They are seen in the right places, where they raise the status of events, and often the charitable income too. They get involved in good causes and politics and lend their name to products. Their latter day lives consist largely of personal appearances.

ANTI-FAME AND VIRTUAL FAME

'Anonymous' is the author of many pages in books of quotations – often for sayings as famous as 'absence makes the heart grow fonder' or 'the singer not the song'. Equally anonymous are the heroes and heroines of folklore – Molly Malone, and the Irene of 'Goodnight Irene'. One of the most famous soldiers is 'The Unknown Soldier'. They are all part of the 'Fanfare for the Common Man' – their very anonymity was a dimension of their fame. To ourselves we are the most important person alive, and the possibility that this importance is shared and reflected by others is some solace to our largely anonymous stay on earth.

More interesting still is the 'virtual fame' of cartoon characters like Tom and Jerry, Mickey Mouse, Donald Duck and the whole stable of Disney and Warner Bros. cartoon figures. These are not even people at all, a paradox cleverly exploited by the film 'Who Killed Roger Rabbit?', where real and cartoon figures meet and interact. The human ability to 'simulate' reality is considered by Richard Dawkins as central to our development: "The evolution of the capacity to simulate seems to have culminated in subjective consciousness. Why this should have happened is, to me, the most profound mystery facing modern biology. Perhaps consciousness arises when the brain's simulation of the world becomes so complete that it must include a model of itself." (Dawkins, 1976)

We have, within the 20th century, simulated much of the real world: synthetic textiles, materials, everyday objects, music, visuals – the list goes on and on. We are steadily improving what Dawkins calls our "survival machines" – robots and artificial intelligence. With the aid of virtual reality we are simulating environments for our virtual heroes to exist in – the pre-history of Jurassic Park, the voyage of the Titanic. Our virtual heroes become cartoon heroes as we explore the world through the eyes of animals ('Bambi'), insects ('A Bug's Life') or children ('Rugrats'). They venture out into space, acquire superhuman powers like Superman, and explore the science fiction world of our future, with its aliens, meteors, space travel, time warps and time machines.

What is remarkable about the whole 20th century is the substitution of fantasy for reality. The real heroes of history are played by the actors of the movie industry. Media reality substitutes for actual reality, as hours of the day are spent in the virtual reality of TV. Fiction substitutes for fact, or interrelates with it in 'infotainment'. Our present day versions of celebrity are media ones – at least two thirds of those we consider famous are the actors, musicians, presenters and entertainers of the media world. Even if in cultural terms our highest awards are the Nobel Prizes, the well known ones are the Oscars, Grammies and Golden Globes. Most of the Nobel prizewinners could walk unnoticed into any restaurant in the world. Few of the Oscar winners could do so without dark glasses and a suitable disguise.

REFERENCES

Boorstin, Daniel (1962) *The Image*, New York

Braudy, Leo (1997) *The Frenzy of Renown – Fame and its History*, NY, Vintage Books

Dawkins, Richard (1976) *The Selfish Gene*, New York, Oxford University Press

Dyer, Richard (1998) *Stars*, London UK, BFI Publishing

Hall, Tony ed. *They Died too Young: The Brief Lives and Tragic Deaths of the Mega-Star legends of Our Time* (the brief lives of 21 remarkable talents, including James Dean Jimi Hendrix, John Lennon, River Phoenix, Elvis Presley, Malcolm X, Marilyn Monroe and Karen Carpenter)

James, Clive (1993) *Fame in the 20th Century*, London UK, BBC Books

Jarvie, IC (1970) *Towards a Sociology of the Cinema*, London, Routledge

Leigh-Kile, Donna (1999) *Sex Symbols*, London, Vision Paperbacks.

Smith, William (1867) *A Classical Dictionary*, London, John Murray

Fame

FAME AND THE MEDIA

"Fame in the ancient world used to be a way of honouring what aspired to be permanent in human action and thought, beyond death and all of life's accidents. Now the word is randomly applied to everything from truly significant events and people to the most fleeting blur in the public eye." (Braudy, 1997)

Welcome to the 20th century – the Media Age. At the end of the second millennium after Christ, we are literally flooded with communication media as radio waves surround us and satellites circle our heads. The glorification of 'celebrity' in such profusion and on all levels down to the trivial may be a new phenomenon, but there have been a number of historical types of 'media' for the preservation of fame, which are in some cases as old as fame itself.

HOW TO TRANSMIT AND KEEP FAME

Fame by definition needs to be preserved – it cannot exist without some form of spreading information. This can be done in many different ways, and through different media. The first musical 'star' can be seen in the cave painting of a musician, circa 18,000 BC. This already tells us that a visual rendering of a person was one of the basic ways of preserving the reputation or fame of that person – exactly the same principal as the pop videos of today. Between then and now we have seen wall and fresco paintings give way to canvas, photography, moving pictures, and finally movies with sound. Three-dimensional preservation of the image of a person ranged from early sculptures to the widespread use of statues to commemorate heroes, methods that have survived to the present day with little basic change. From earliest times comes embalming, and the traditions of the Egyptians have survived into the 20th century with the embalmed bodies of Lenin and Stalin. The oral tradition of fame survived within communities and cultures, but was better transmitted by hieroglyphs, then alphabetical words, then printing. In this way, books, poems, sagas and epics were passed down. Some of these were memoirs, autobiographies and personal creeds of great men – Caesar, Alexander, Lenin, Stalin, Mao, Hitler. Music was added to create songs and ballads, immortalising both the already known and the otherwise unknown, like Tom Dooley.

Fame was also, from earliest times, communicated through a range of objects that guaranteed wide circulation. Coins, banknotes and stamps were widely used to disseminate the fame of rulers and heroes. Later objects included cars, sometimes with famous names like Lincoln, sometimes carrying the name of their originator, like Ferrari, or of the women associated with the originator like Mercedes (the daughter of Benz, who himself gave his name to benzene). Sometimes the object never surpassed its creator, like the Mae West lifejacket, the Peach Melba or the Caesar Salad. But often the object would become more famous than the person it was named after – the Eiffel Tower, the sandwich, even the Betty Ford Clinic.

Fame clearly could be bought with money, provided the initial concept was good enough, as in a landmark or a successful clinic. Prizes and bursaries proliferated, serving alike those who desired fame and those who desired money. Some prizes became famous, like the Nobel and Pulitzer prizes. But probably few people today would know much, or indeed anything, about Alfred Nobel or Joseph Pulitzer – two good examples of self-made men who acquired great wealth and power. They might well have sacrificed fame for physical immortality. But not dying has never been an option, whereas immortality through fame has always been a possibility for those who were clever with their power and money. Names such as Carnegie, Fulbright, Wolfson and Rockefeller live on through their bequests more than their actual works. The same motivation that drove such men to transcend the limits of ordinary lives clearly drove them to transcend the limits of death itself.

THE RECORDING OF ARTISTIC TALENT

There has always been a crucial interrelation between the art and the medium that records it. On the one hand artists, like scientists and inventors, have sought to manipulate or improve existing media, or create new ones like photography and sound recordings. On the other hand, the particular media that existed at various points in history have fashioned the creative possibilities of the artist.

The simplest distinction is between the creative and the perform-ing artist. The creative artist had, from cave walls onwards, a variety of long lasting media suitable for recording his or her work. The result is that creative artists found it easy to find fame – artists, architects, composers, writers are well preserved to the present day. Another useful benefit of such longevity is that artists who were unappreciated in their own time can be re-assessed within the fullness of time, and in the case of Van Gogh, become the 'highest earning' artist ever in terms of the present value of their oevre. Very few performers, however, are remembered at all before the 20th century, and even those with reputations as large as Liszt or Paganini cannot be judged against their latter-day fellows.

All that changed with the advent of sound and film recording. Performers became the stars of the popular musical world to the point that two of Madonna's songwriters were not even invited to meet her – they were not considered significant enough to be given access. The 'authors' of the music business may get money from sales but only the greatest such as Gershwin, Porter or Bacharach achieve fame. Often singer-songwriters are more famous as singers than songwriters – as with Joni Mitchell or Bob Dylan. The personality of the performers became as important as their artistic output, and this cult of personality spread from the popular music world to the classical, resulting in Herbert Von Karajan's name appearing in bigger type than the composer's by the end of his career.

The dominance of the 'personality with charisma' grew with the visual media, where the image replaced the physical person and took on a new life of its own. That this was possible relied on our psychological ability to physically reconstruct in our minds a 'personality' from a set of visual details – something people have done over the ages through phrenology or visual stereotyping. There is no doubt that seeing people made the biggest difference in fame – the old photographs of the Wild West gave us unforgettable portraits of outlaws, native American chiefs and the first American heroes. Photos of such as Lenin, Stalin, Einstein and Lincoln became universally known, and were even used as marketing symbols.

Nowhere was the advent of the famous performer more evident than in the movie age, when screen images began to move and then talk. The focus of fame finally shifted away from the 'creators' – studio chiefs like Goldwyn and Mayer, directors like Hitchcock, Bergman and Eisenstein and the authors and scriptwriters of films – to the 'ordinary person' who was elevated through screen stardom to a status that transcended the creative process itself. Directors performed themselves, in order to take advantage of the fame accorded to the image on screen, making stars out of Orson Welles and Woody Allen. Even Hitchcock sneaked into every one of his own films. The new performers of the movie age changed the entire profile of fame. As the decades of the 20th century moved on this new type of fame – that of a person who had done nothing noteworthy in real life but impersonate the characters of fiction – began to elbow out the famous names of history, such as politicians, inventors or explorers. The media had started to show its power in the new electronic age.

MEDIUM AND MESSAGE IN THE AGE OF ELECTRONICS

One factor which has typified the 20th century is the explosion of different forms of electronic media – moving pictures, sound recording, radio, television, digital media, computers, virtual reality, games consoles, telephones, faxes and emails. New media seem to be waiting just round the corner. In 1967, at the apex of the 60s renaissance, where new sounds and images jostled together to stun the 'youth generation', Marshall McLuhan wrote a ground-breaking book 'The Medium is the Massage'. This presented to the public in a visually arresting way a phenomenon they were rapidly getting to know more of – the power of the 'medium' itself:

"The medium, or process, of our time – electronic technology – is reshaping and restructuring patterns of social interdependence and every aspect of our personal life. Everything is changing dramatically. Societies have always been shaped more by the nature of the media by which men communicate than by the content of the communication. It is impossible to understand social and cultural changes without a knowledge of the workings of media. Youth instinctively understands the present environment – the electric drama. It lives mythically and in depth." (McLuhan and Fiore, 1967)

The term 'mythically and in depth' catches very well the way in which audiences responded to film and TV technology. And since 1967, many aspects of the content of movies have changed as a result of ongoing developments in hardware. First, the video recorder enabled home viewing. This increased dramatically – in 1980 film revenue from cinemas was 80% whereas by 1990 this had already dropped to 30%. At about the same time came that very underestimated 'shaper' of home viewing – the hand held remote control unit. For the first time, this enabled the viewer to flick between channels instantaneously, to browse rapidly through several choices and then to stop at whatever caught the eye. This trend would favour outdoor action movies with stunts, or anything visually or sonically arresting, or anything with a lot of action per second. Rapid browsing would mitigate against 'narrative' movies which had slower plot development and more meaningful conversation, unless the viewer was deliberately seeking such material. Films such as 'Die Hard', in fact, achieved their major success not on cinema release but in post-cinema video sales, illustrating the trend for action videos to be extensively bought or rented for home viewing.

The show-and-tell trend in movies was wonderfully caught in the film 'The Last Tycoon' in the scene where the Irving Thalberg-like movie mogul Monroe Starr (Robert de Niro) 'shows' the over-wordy screenwriter (played by Donald Pleasance) how to develop a gripping plot in a purely visual way (the scriptwriting here being the work of the marvellously economic and elliptical Harold Pinter). It illustrates the point made by Nina Foch: "When I was a girl in Hollywood, a script would have pages and pages of talk. We forgot that we were in moving pictures." (March 27, 1984, in McClelland, 1986). McLuhan pointed to the same thing in 1967, in relation to TV: "Television completes the cycle of the human sensorium. With the omnipresent ear and the moving eye, we have abolished writing. But the visual is only one component in a complex interplay. The images wrap around you. You are the screen, the vanishing point. The main cause for criticism of television is the failure on the part of its critics to view it as a totally new technology which demands different sensory responses. These critics insist on regarding television as merely a degraded form of print technology." (McLuhan and Fiore, 1967)

There is another good reason for little dialogue and strong visuals. If we look at the psychological profile of the general population, we see that 'imaginative' (Intuitive) types, who are able to supply fantasy from within their own heads – and create it in the films they make – are outnumbered over two to one by 'realistic' (Sensing) types, who have a greater need for the fantasy content to be provided externally for them by the plot and visuals of the film itself. As they want 'convenience food', so they want 'convenience viewing', where all the creative preparation has been done, and all that remains is to consume the product. Another interesting feature of the 'realistic' type is its preference for tried and tested solutions rather than experimentation (Myers and Myers, 1980). This preference might explain why a public that has enjoyed a film such as 'Rocky', 'Naked Gun' or 'Police Academy' then flock to see sequel after sequel, and why they happily put up with 'the familiar' in terms of actors, plots, locations and even dialogue.

DUMBING DOWN – THE UNIMPORTANCE OF BEING A SCRIPTWRITER.

" 'It is totally impossible to make a great picture out of a lousy script,' says the veteran filmmaker Billy Wilder. And yet, if good screen plays are so sought after, why is it that writers are treated like third class citizens?"(Kent, 1991)

Hollywood screenwriters typically work in pairs to bounce ideas and try out dialogue, and there may be as many as eight different pairs of writers on any one production. But only a small number will get credits, and even this may only be with the help and pressure of their Union lawyers. Screenwriters were thrown out of Hollywood in their numbers during the McCarthy years, and one of the great scriptwriters, SJ Perelman, quipped that he was going to live in Britain because he had heard that "politeness there was only skin deep". When people looked nonplussed he added "and after Hollywood that's deep enough for me".

The unimportance of the screenwriter is not total – Joe Eszterhas was paid $3 million for his script to 'Basic Instinct' (though he was off the project less than two months after the sale) and figures of $1 million for scripts are not uncommon. But money is not the same as importance in a world where 'show and tell' easily outranks 'tell'. If visual effects have, in some cases, broken new boundaries ('2001', 'Jurassic Park') that define the cinema as a true art form, in most cases they have rarely strayed beyond the typical 'outdoor action' formulae of cops, robbers, aliens, car chases, smoke-spewing explosions and languid close-ups of dewy eyed lovers. The script deemed necessary to accompany such formulaic visuals has its own telling ring – where have we heard expressions such as 'I'm a good cop', 'Trust me', 'I love you' and 'let's get outta here' before? Yet again, it is the tried and tested that appeals to the majority 'realistic' psychological profile in the population.

Welcome to dumbing down, and the cosiness of appealing to the lowest common denominator in the audience. The effect on stars is to demote the speaking voice (resurrected in voice-overs and documentary narrative in the case of Orson Welles and Raymond Burr) in favour of a photogenic face for close-ups, an impeccable sense of timing and the ability to show emotion to camera. Great actors like Vincent Price and Sir Laurence Olivier – who could mesmerise theatres in their own right – survived on film because of their charisma and sheer technique, not their magnificent voices. Often the dialogue was simply the basis of the overall effect they were able to create by the full use of their considerable talents. When stars were cast in films with great dialogue, such as those of Tennessee Williams ('Cat on a Hot Tin Roof', 'A Streetcar named Desire', 'The Glass Menagerie', 'Suddenly last Summer') the results could be memorable, but these were not the big box office blockbusters. Schwarzenegger's voice may be perfect for lines such as "hasta la vista baby", but the greatest star of the present-day box office would hardly be first choice for sophisticated narrative. And without such narrative (hardly something eight teams of scriptwriters working in rotation are likely to create) there is unlikely to be true psychological depth of character.

Sometimes the dumbing down is done in good faith by actors in order to make it more flexible and easier to act, but this is again not without its perils: "When Phil Alden Robinson sold a story called 'Rhinestone' to Twentieth Century Fox, the studio allowed its star Sylvester Stallone to rewrite virtually every word of the script. The movie bombed. Robinson admits that it is almost impossible for a writer to protect his or her work. Unfortunately for professional screen-writers, almost everyone in Hollywood (studio executives, stars, directors and producers) is under the illusion that they can write. Writing screenplays may seem easy but writing them well is as difficult as anything you can imagine." (Kent, 1991) The enormous changes made to scripts by teams of people has caused the optimistic to view the original script as simply a 'blueprint' for which there are many more rewriters than writers. It is only made into cinematographic art during the process of filming.

Following the principle that a camel is a horse designed by a committee, the end product will rarely be a thoroughbred with an established lineage. What is likely to happen is that the good screen-writers will spend more time arguing than writing, while the stock ones will spend the creative meetings simply listening to the will of the direc-tor. Truffaut's premise, that it is the director who is the true 'auteur' of the film, whilst in vogue at one stage, failed to either improve the dialogue or replace the talent of original writers such as Raymond Chandler or Ben Hecht. As Garson Kanin put it: "It is inevitable that the writer be subservient to the director. As filmmaking became more complex and sophisticated, people were hired to write scripts, but never were they considered other than hired talent. It was not unusual on the lot to hear directors refer to a screenwriter as 'my writer'. This tradition exists to this day." (Films in Review, Nov. 1974, in McClelland, 1986). The down side of this is described by Waldo Salt: "In the old days at least they tried to get people like Dorothy Parker and William Faulkner to work for them, then they'd mess up the writing. Now, people see scripts as talking papers to get a hot star or director interested in a package. It's a question of priorities." (The New York Times Magazine, Oct 23, 1983, in McClelland, 1986).

The show and tell style of movie has a number of knock-on effects on the type of star it favours. Because of the relatively low importance of dialogue, much has to be suggested by close-ups of the star, so the star has to be visually charismatic, and able to suggest a large range of emotion without words. Eyes are important, and enhanced by cosmetics and different lenses to change colour. So also is the mouth and the bone structure and profile of the face, which have become the subject of increasing plastic surgery. The ability to deliver long speeches is less required, so the theatrical techniques of pacing speeches and using rhetoric are declining. The increase in action content requires a fitter and stronger star, so male and female stars work out in gyms. The male star may be required to look strong for certain roles, so muscle bulk and tone may also be relevant. A sense of humour is required to portray the irony and psychological depth that may not be explicitly provided in the dialogue. If we put together these requirements we have the archetypal stars of today – Sylvester Stallone and Arnold Schwarzenegger.

THE MEDIA AS A POWER BASE – HOW IT SELECTS THE FAMOUS

One effect of the rise of the media (film, TV, Radio, newspapers and magazines) in the last hundred years is the choice of celebrity or star that the media considers newsworthy and, therefore, keeps in front of the public. Those who feature in current box office successes in the US are rarely out of the public eye. Stars like Stallone and

Fame and the Media

Schwarzenegger, and their musical equivalents, have the benefit of extensive publicity and merchandising and will be backed by important multinational conglomerates with syndicated media interests like Sony or Warner. Alongside the multinational stars, there are the national stars and celebrities, politicians and sportspeople of each particular country.

The media's choice of celebrities can be seen in the obituaries they feature at the end of each year. If we look at the 1998 obituaries in the Sunday Express and The Sunday Times, for instance, we see that about two thirds are people from the entertainment world (70% in The Express, 62% in The Times, including 10% musicians in The Express and 16% in The Times). The rest is made up of sportspeople (10% in both) and politicians (6% in The Express, 16% in The Times) and then a smattering of discoverers, inventors and miscellaneous others who had at one time or another featured in the news. The only difference with the 'serious' broadsheet newspapers, such as The Times, is that a small number of media celebrities are replaced with politicians – the sport content stays the same. Much the same trend can be seen with Cosmopolitan's list of 'Men We Love', where 80% are from the entertainment world (including 18% musicians), 10% are sportsmen and 7% are politicians (omitting people from the fashion world as particular to Cosmo readership).

So, at the end of the 20th century, when we talk of 'fame' we are talking about a heavy bias to the celebrities of the media world – the Hollywood stars, the national TV celebrities, the big musical acts. We then have the sportspeople – our contemporary 'strongest and fastest' – down at 10%. But the politicians, who have traditionally been the heroes of history, barely match the sportspeople in fame. It is worth pointing out that in today's world there are almost no monarchs with any power. Politicians in democratic countries are frequently changed every five years (or less in some countries like Italy), so the chance of their doing enough in their lives to be truly famous is far less likely than it was in the past. And despite their modest achievements, politicians generally lack the charisma that keeps media stars like Marilyn Monroe or Elvis Presley alive in the hearts of the people.

The interests of the media in creating and manipulating fame have gradually increased towards the self-publicising of its own members. The 1998 Sunday Times obituaries included four newspaper figures out of its total of 77. Braudy takes a cynical view of the media's involvement in creating news. "These days a great proportion of what the media considers to be news is its own effect on people and events. Since the nineteenth century the experiences of war correspondents have been part of the events they report. Now, reporters standing outside the home of a person in the spotlight interview one another as they wait for the appearance of the nominal centre of attention. The media are no longer only what their name implies: intermediaries between events and audiences. Now, a metamedia has come into being, committed to, imprisoned by, and frequently bored to death by its own preoccupation with fame." (Braudy, 1997)

Braudy's view of the media as knowingly influential in affecting the course of events is tempered by the total confusion he attributes to them in trying to establish what fame actually means. It is a process in which he and similar experts are constantly asked for 'interpretations' by the press (something which largely motivated our own book): "In a world overcrowded with people, places, things and ideas, the problem of what deserves attention is a crucial issue. Fame in modern society has thereby become a common language, the credo of the media as well as their basic subject matter: who ought to be famous, who shouldn't, whom we have forgotten, who ought to be remembered. Always the questions are posed in terms of specific events and individuals. But the real curiosity is about the media's role in the processes of fame: How do you get it? How do you keep it? How do you lose it? Why are we so fascinated by famous people?" (Braudy, 1997)

Braudy's further explanation of why the media turns to 'experts' is that they want the inside story – not necessarily the truth, but simply a hidden depth that others are not aware of. When Clinton avoids the issue on TV, journalists turn to body language experts. When assessing as yet unproven guilt or innocence they turn to criminal psychologists. When trying to establish whether video nasties cause copycat behaviour they turn to media psychologists. Armed with the opinions of the media experts, they then set about writing the so-called hidden stories and buried angles.

THE CRITIC

The self-publicising of the press turns to iconisation in the media award ceremonies such as the UK Press Awards or the PTA Awards for magazine journalism, which they – as did the music industry – borrowed from Hollywood. Attempts to raise journalists or editors to cult status, however, have met with little response from the public despite their elevation to the media obituaries. The critic is one phenomenon that represents what the press would like to aspire to in increasing its profile and power base. Often dismissed as a 'failed performer', the critic usually justifies his or her existence by the claim that the public is ignorant in two ways: ignorant of true standards of taste and aesthetics, and ignorant of actual works they have not yet seen or heard.

The essential use of the critic is to describe a work or production. The self declared mission of the critic, however, is often to guide public taste. This grandiose task can fail on several counts. First, the critic who can safely say 'I personally do or do not like this aspect or that aspect', may want to go further and say 'this is objectively good or bad', which is another matter entirely. Second, the public en masse (known as the box-office in the movies) may and frequently does prove the critic wrong, by supporting works dismissed as not worth seeing. This is well known in the business. "The screenwriter William Goldman has famously said of movie people that 'Nobody knows anything'. But everyone in Hollywood knows what sells a movie. It's called 'word of mouth'. If a friend recommends a movie the odds are pretty good that you will act on that recommendation." (Kent, 1991) Third, how do we define 'good'? Do we agree with Harold Robbins who, whilst he was the biggest selling contemporary author, declared that if he was the most popular he must be the best?

Besides all of the above, many famous critics had notoriously fragile egos. Not only were they often angry with the world and its inhabitants, but they were also open to influence by flattery and rejection, as Ray Milland remembers: "Wise Hollywood hostesses never invited columnists (like Luella Parsons or Hedda Hopper) to their parties, because once you did you could never leave them off your list for future parties or they would crucify you." (Milland, 1974) Hopper put it more succinctly, pointing to her home in Beverley Hills and boasting "That's the house that fear built." When Merle Oberon asked her why she had written such vicious things about her she replied "Bitchery, dear, sheer bitchery." (Boller and Davis, 1987)

At its best, the work of critics like Dorothy Parker or George Bernard Shaw is literature in its own right. At worst, the relationship between critics and their victims can degenerate into outright war. Such incidents occurred when Joan Bennett sent Hopper a live skunk in a hatbox, and when British playwright John Osborne formed a circle of fellow writers whose sole declared intention was to destroy and humiliate critics in retaliation for their attacks on writers. The critic, however, remains one of the elements in the definition of the star and of what degree of fame that star will enjoy. Critics are more feared by actors than their ability to make or break people probably merits. This may have a lot to do with the superstition of actors, and the passive role they have to suffer both off the set in waiting to be cast and on the set in acting to a director.

The worst effects of critics throughout history have doubtless been not in what they actually said, but in the self doubt they generated within the heads of those actors, musicians and others they criticised, which led in many cases to depression and prolonged periods off work. Famous people living on the highest pinnacle of celebrity are all too aware that their gifts may be overrated by the media and public, and secretly – to a greater or lesser extent – feel that they are 'a fraud' and will one day be found out. It may not need much from a critic to persuade the star that that day has come.

USE AND ABUSE OF STARS IN THE MEDIA

"Princess Diana learned early on that by manipulating the media she could endear herself to the British and then the world public. Her relationship with the Press and theirs with her was a mutual feeding frenzy, which was hugely successful for both sides. It gave her the strength to stand up to the Royal family and made her the biggest star in the world", states publicist Max Clifford. (Leigh-Kile, 1999) However, the media itself has said, in the person of author and editor Richard Barber, "In the loosest sense I believe we all contributed to Diana's death. The paparazzi didn't kill her. What killed her was a man more than three times over the legal drink limit, unable to handle the Mercedes. But one of the reasons he was driving too fast was that that Diana had acquired the reputation of being the most famous person in the world and was being hounded wherever she went." (Leigh-Kile, 1999)

Given the collusion between the star, the publicist and the media, who do we blame for abuses? Who, for instance is behind the hyped up image of Vanessa Mae as a 'sex symbol', Charlotte Church as a 'child prodigy', Nigel Kennedy as a 'rebel' or Liam Gallagher as 'the bad boy of pop'? Is it implicit in their nature, is it purely marketing or is it deemed to be what the public wants in order to fulfil their own entertainment needs? Certainly the hyping of the image is a thriving business within the fame industry. PR itself is as old as the hills – Paul did one of the best PR jobs in history in spreading the story of Jesus. But how does marketing turn to hype, and hype then turn into pure inventions like 'Freddy Starr ate my Hamster'?

Publicist Max Clifford, who floated the 'hamster' myth in the British press, is open about the way stories are invented in the media: "In the 60s you could get away with murder. I could say, for instance, 'The Beatles sold 50,000 albums this week' when they sold five. No one would check. I had no misgivings about making up stories because it gave the press something bigger and better to generate. What's the truth anyway? I can take any newspaper today and think 'well, we have a little substance here, but that's a load of rubbish'. Trying to draw the line between reality and fiction is impossible. I have worked with stars and given them story lines and a year later they repeat them back to me. Then I have to remind them, 'Hold on, don't you remember? I made that up.' Sometimes they know they are lying but often they don't. We're not dealing in reality. It's virtual reality. It's infotainment – information as entertainment."(Leigh-Kile, 1999)

TRUTH, LIES AND 'INFOTAINMENT'

As Donna Leigh-Kile points out, "Stars inhabit a surreal world where fact, fiction and fantasy collide. We see them posing "at home" in houses that have been borrowed for the photo shoot. We read their fabricated life stories. Some of it may be fact, some of it may not. But ultimately in this world of infotainment it is not important. What matters is to be true to the image." (Leigh-Kile, 1999)

On the one hand we have the media, with the active collusion of the stars themselves, manipulating and changing the truth. On the other hand we have the public. Do they want the truth or do they themselves want this phenomenon of 'infotainment'? In some crucial cases – like the OJ Simpson trial, they themselves seem to have preferred the 'sanitised' star to the real human being. This is especially the case where the public accepts the persona as the person and blocks out anything that does not fit the image: "When actress Sondra Locke wrote her kiss-and-tell book about Clint Eastwood it did not sell well because, according to film academic Jeanine Basinger, people had already made their minds about him from seeing his films. As an icon, Eastwood's reputation is unassailable."(Leigh-Kile, 1999)

The phenomenon of 'infotainment' is crucial to the fame industry, and dates from what is considered to be the very creation of the 'star' phenomenon. This pivotal event was itself crucially built on deception: "The key event in this history, and the event cited as 'creating a movie star' for the first time is usually taken to be Carl Laemmle's action of planting a story in the St. Louis Post-Dispatch to the effect that Florence Lawrence, up to then known by the 'studio' name as the "Biograph Girl", had been killed by a trolley car in St. Louis, and following it a day later with an advertisement in the trade press denouncing the story as a vicious lie. This event was the first occasion that a film actor's name became known to the public. It is the first example of the deliberate manufacture of a star's image. Equally, runs the argument, it is the first example of the producers of films responding to public demand, giving the public what it wanted. It is thus at the point of intersection of public demand (the star as a phenomenon of consumption) and the producer initiative (the star as a phenomenon of production)." (Dyer, 1998). Ominously, as a portent of the history of stars, truth and the cinema to come, Lawrence committed suicide in 1938 while Laemmle went on to found Universal Studios.

If both the media and the public collude to produce fantasy instead of truth, then what value does truth have? Truth may be purely optional in the fantasy world of the movies, but stars are two things: vehicles for the fictitious and real people. While virtual reality may be an 'amoral' state of affairs, human beings can undergo actual suffering, which is a moral state of affairs.

REFERENCES

Braudy, Leo (1997) *The Frenzy of Renown – Fame and its History*, NY, Vintage Books

Dyer, Richard (1998) *Stars*, London, British Film Institute Publishing

Kent, Nicolas (1991) *Naked Hollywood*, London, BBC Books

Leigh-Kile, Donna (1999) *Sex Symbols*, London, Vision Paperbacks.

McClelland, Doug (1985) *Hollywood on Hollywood – Tinsel Town Talks* Winchester MA USA:

McLuhan, M and Fiore, Q(1967) *The Medium is the Massage*, London, Penguin Books

Milland, Ray (1974) *Wide-Eyed in Babylon*

Myers, IB and Myers, PB (1980) *Gifts Differing*, Palo Alto, Consulting Psychologists Press

Fame

STARS AND THEIR AUDIENCES

The concept of the star first grew out of the theatre world. In the mid 19th century, larger theatres started to replace the smaller companies, and the reputations created by some of the better actors allowed these theatres to sell more seats. Improvements in travel meant that once an actor became well known, he or she could tour – in the US as well as in Europe. As a result, certain star players began to stand out from the usual stock companies, and then toured in the same star role from one city to the next with a locally hired cast. The star profile then diversified to include certain stereotypical characters – the juvenile, the comedian, and the leading man and woman. Reputations began to travel and grow with these new stars. The theatres then fell into the hands of businessmen who made money out of the new stars by allowing productions to run for as long as the people came. This signalled the start of money replacing art as the determining factor in what shows were put on. Syndicates started to buy chains of theatres and became particularly strong in the US.

Moving pictures started with the inventions of the self-operated Kinetoscope in 1889. This was followed in 1896 by the Vitascope, a primitive projection unit, and then the more sophisticated all day Nickelodeon shows in 1905. With the advent of the Cinema, with more expensive tickets and feature pictures several reels long, the power of the syndicates became huge. A theatre star could physically be in only one place at a time. On film his or her image could be anywhere where one could set up a projection unit. It was through moving pictures and the longer feature films that the creation of the huge stars of today became possible.

Why was the use of the star so dramatically increased in the Hollywood Movies? Dyer (1998) suggests that there were crucial economic determinants:

Capital – stars represented a form of capital held by the studios, or to put it another way a kind of monopoly based on the uniqueness of each individual star.

Investment – stars were a guarantee against loss on an investment, and hopefully also a guarantee of profit on it.

Outlay – Stars were a substantial portion of a film's budget that they had to act in such a way that would safeguard the outlay.

The Market – Stars were used to sell films and organise the market, also using the quality of their star status to enhance the perceived content of the film itself.

Hortense Powdermaker in her 'anthropological investigation' of Hollywood, 'The Dream Factory', puts it thus: "The star has tangible features which can be advertised and marketed, and can be 'typed' as the villain, hero, siren, sweet young girl, neurotic woman. The system provides a formula easy to understand and may serve also to protect executives from having to pay too much attention to such intangibles as the quality of a story or of acting. Here is a standardised product which can be sold and which banks regard as insurance for large profits." (Powdermaker, 1950)

THE FINANCIAL POWER OF THE STAR

To the public there are many stars, superstars and megastars – terms used uncritically and indiscriminately. There is, however, another considerably narrower and more precise definition which is used by the financial part of the industry. The difference between the star (Tom Cruise, Eddie Murphy) and the great actor (Robert De Niro, Meryl Streep), is the ability to sell movies or more specifically to open a movie. 'Opening a movie' is Hollywood slang for the ability to entice sufficient numbers of people to see the movie during its first weekend to merit the placing of a double page, full colour advertisement in Daily Variety.

"During the summer (traditional blockbuster time) of 1990, a succession of such ads celebrated the opening grosses scored by Tom Cruise in 'Days of Thunder' ($21.5 million over five days), Eddie Murphy in 'Another 48 Hours' ($19.5 million over three days), Michael J Fox in 'Back to the Future, Part III' ($23.7 million over four days) and Arnold Schwarzenegger in 'Total Recall' ($25.5 million on its opening weekend). The studio bosses who have invested between $30 million and $60 million in what they hope will be that summer's big movie pore over these opening weekend figures with the feverish curiosity of men who know that they are reading a prognosis of their own careers. If you want some security about making a $30 million investment, it would be very nice to have Danny De Vito or Michael Douglas or Robert Redford on the other end of that camera." (Kent, 1991).

Note also that when we talk of opening a movie, we are also talking strictly men, and not so long ago that would also have been white men. And when women sell more than men (Cameron Diaz and Julia Roberts

are not too far off), it will be women opening movies, as the only crite-
rion is money – pure and simple. The power of the star, as typical
salaries per movie pass $20 million and keep rising, has increasingly
started to rival that of the studio. In fact co-ownership deals between
star and studio, not a new idea (United Artists was founded in 1919 by
Fairbanks, Chaplin and Pickford to gain control over their careers) but
increasingly viable when stars are worth millions, spreads both the
financial risk and the profits. "If the terms of the deal work out then
everybody's happy. Universal's blockbuster comedy, 'Twins', made
more than $110 million at the American box office and only cost the
studio $18 million to make. When the time came to divide up the prof-
its, (about 40 per cent of the box office take), Universal had to stand in
line behind Schwarzenegger (17.5 per cent), De Vito and director Ivan
Reitman." (Kent, 1991)

David Shipman attributes much of the power of the stars to the
dramatic rise in bargaining power of their agents, which has surpassed
that of the movie moguls of the studio contract days. "By common
consent, Mike Ovitz of Creative Artists Agency is the most powerful
man in Hollywood; the other agencies with the most prestigious list of
clients are William Morris and ICM. There are never enough talented
writers, directors or stars: the agents influence the creative personnel
about their career choices. They are also responsible for getting them
huge fees. Today the actors demand a chauffeur and a limo before
they've read the script." (Shipman, 1991)

Another reason star salaries escalate is that there are, according to
Ned Tanen (ex-studio chief at Universal and then Paramount), not
many actors in Hollywood considered to have 'box office' star status.
"There are a lot of people who are paid like movie stars but there are
really only half a dozen movie stars in this world and it is very difficult
to get them to work. Since we are no longer living in the contract era
of the twenties and thirties and forties, you don't own these people. If
they turn you down your choices get more and more limited. So you
pay the best people you can three, four, five million dollars. In many
cases you are overpaying for what you are getting but you end up talking yourself into going with these people who may be incredibly gifted
actors and actresses but they don't sell tickets." (Kent, 1991)

Stars were reputed to have saved whole studios at crucial times –
Mae West at Paramount and Deanna Durbin at Universal in 1937.

However, they could also backfire and fail to prevent huge losses on big budget turkeys like 'Cleopatra'. With the progress towards realism in the movies, more and more films do well at the box office despite having no great stars ('Reservoir Dogs', 'The Full Monty'). So while stars are not necessary, they are still preferred by those that finance the media industry – most of all the multinationals to whom they are signed – and so the phenomenon, once created, has lasted unabated.

This is as true in the music industry as it is in films. In both cases the fabrication of stars has been pursued with a zeal that stretched as far as the merchandising of a whole range of products built around the star. The money involved in this merchandising is attested to by the cut-throat patent wars over the legacies of Princess Diana and Elvis Presley. It is also no surprise that Schwarzenegger, who "talks about his own career as if he were a brand name product and exploits his name with the same dedication that the fast food chain devotes to the international exploitation of ground meat" (Kent, 1991) has a Business Studies background. It is also no surprise that, like Madonna, he has an infinite capacity for the kind of hard work that is essential to self promotion, having trained for five hours a day to become number one in the bodybuilding world. Like Madonna, he is so financially astute that he works from within the industry itself to generate new promotional roles and material. This is the definition, if you like, of the star as the 'phenomenon of production'.

Edgar Morin is one who takes the view that the fabrication of a star image conceals little actual substance: "Stars do not have a strong character, but a definable, publicisable personality: a figure which can become a nationally advertised trademark. The qualities which now commonly make a man or woman into a 'nationally advertised' brand are in fact a new category of human emptiness." (Morin, 1960) Daniel Boorstin explains the 'ordinariness' of many stars by our general satisfaction and smugness with our contemporary culture, in which we elevate the commonplace ('Forrest Gump') rather than looking for the ground breaking or extraordinary. He sees movie stereotypes as not even defining our social values in a deeper or artistic way, but often merely stating what is. "The typical becomes the ideal, the average the best. The cultural predecessors of stars – the artist, the prostitute, the adulteress, the great criminal and outcast, the warrior, the rebel-poet, the devil, the fool are 'essentially transformed' into the vamp, the national hero, the neurotic housewife, the gangster, the charismatic tycoon. They are no longer images of another way of life but rather freaks of the same life, serving as an affirmation of the established order." (Boorstin, 1963) This pessimistic viewpoint is in keeping with the concept of stars as pure manipulations of their multinational owners. It does not, however, explain what psychological factors communicate with the public and make them identify with their stars in a positive way.

The use of the camera close up enabled the viewpoint of the audience to be so close that a new level of intimacy was possible. We can intrude on a person's private world as only a lover would be able to do in a sexual way, or as a family member in an emotional way, to touch or hug or wipe away tears. The close up is one of the ways in which the public could form a psychological bond with the star, and was also a key part of the audience fantasy – that the star likes us and consequently invites us up close. We imagine the star likes us because we like the star, and the star is portrayed in such a way as to be likeable, sometimes despite many faults. Even the faults can have their role, as the victim appeals to the rescuer in us. The close up can dramatise at will any of the three roles of the Drama Triangle (Berne, 1973). This is shown below:

The Drama happens when the roles switch over, as when the persecutor turns into a rescuer, or the victim turns into the persecutor. The audience may, for example, feel like rescuing the victim being persecuted by something huge like King Kong, but then switch their sympathy to the ape as he poignantly perishes in the final reel. In the numerous film and TV plots concerning injustice (many based on real cases), the victims get their revenge in the courtroom. Comedy is often based on sudden and unexpected switches, and this was one of the key dynamics of duos like Laurel and Hardy. It is also the basis of the Tom and Jerry cartoons, where the plot consists of endless switches between victim and persecutor as one or other has the upper hand, with occasional moments of rescue as one or the other feels guilty. The popular conception about comedy simply making fun of victims ignores both the tension of juxtaposing two opposite states and the switch that sparks off the humour. Many of these elements are best seen in close up, as the camera tracks the switches in mood of the characters.

The close up is also a way of proving that star quality is not based on purely physical beauty but on the expression of the face, and that expression is the communication of the personality within. This is even true of supermodels. Sixties British icon Celia Hammond remembers that her contemporary models were "surprisingly intelligent" – hardly surprising in fact, since intelligence can be a crucial part of personal magnetism. It seems surprising only in the sense that many such intelligent models and dancers have traditionally been treated only as bodies (or infantilised as 'girls', the insider term for models).

It is simple to show that the act of thought, and the emotions accompanying it, are crucial to physical presence by the fact that a statue – while well proportioned – has no dynamic personality because no thought is passing through it. Many hopeful girls believe quite falsely that their bodies alone can make them stars. And the tradition of treating models as purely physical images may also be responsible for the problems girls who imitate them have with weight reduction and eventually anorexia. The truth is that it is a very special aura and personality that gives a certain look. Models who have been rocketed to fame overnight may say they were lucky to be in the right place at the right time, but they already had a physical presence strong enough to magnetise the gazes of the agency staff and photographers who crossed their paths. As British journalist Peter Yorke put it, "If beauty isn't genius it usually signals at least a high level of animal cunning." (London Collection Magazine, 1978)

The importance of personality over body is illustrated by Celia Hammond's overnight rise to fame. She was a stone overweight when discovered and was only given two weeks to lose it before being flown over to France to model the Paris collections. Even then, she was told at the start of her modelling career that "she didn't have the legs to make it" and laboured under that unfortunate curse for a good two years. Her art was that of 'looking good to camera', and in art there is technique, and in technique there is intelligence. As Rossetti said, "Conception, fundamental brainwork is what makes the difference in all art." (Letter to Hall Caine in Caine, 1882) The art of acting to camera is the foundation of Michael Caine's uncanny 'presence', and the misconception that he just 'acts himself' was firmly refuted by his classic training video on the techniques involved in this.

The definition of the star as someone with extraordinary personal qualities and presence negates the concept of the star as simply glorifying the ordinary. There is a particular parameter of personal magnetism that is also socially rebellious – the parameter of challenge. On one level, challenge is seen in flirting whilst on another it is seen in anarchic humour. It can be seen in sexual experimentation, groundbreaking fashion, swearing in the media, even antisocial and criminal acts. Rebellion against the so-called established order is a crucial trait in the creative formula (Evans, 1994) and has been well documented in all the literature relating to creativity. Those who try to become stars by following convention may completely miss the point that true 'star quality' may derive from challenging or flaunting convention.

OVERNIGHT FAME – THE DOCUSOAPS

A recent phenomenon which has taken media realism one step further is the docusoap; a soap opera in several episodes featuring members of the public as the stars. Does this then confirm Boorstin's pessimistic view of not defining our social values in a deeper or artistic way, but merely 'stating what is'? In the sense that these are real people captured on camera in the course of their 'ordinary lives', there seems a lot of truth in this. Certainly some of the docusoap celebrities – the atrocious drivers seen by surveillance video in car chases for instance – are somewhere near the Boorstin definition of "freaks of the established order".

But is he right that "The typical becomes the ideal, the average the best?" Not if what is required for the success of the docusoap is the emergence of a star personality from the general public (which is the pool from which many Hollywood stars were discovered in the first place). Where this is the case, the star is once again someone with a presence strong and original enough to stand out from the general public, needing only a lucky break and some good PR to go on to a genuine media career, as the majority of docusoap stars have done. And if we look at the personalities of the stars that stand out in the docusoaps, we find it is the creative and rebellious ones (Maureen Rees in 'Driving School', Jeremy Spake in 'Airport') who do not define the typical or the average, but yet again deviate from it. We might not go so far as Samuel Goldwyn in claiming movie stars were made by God, but we might agree with the statement that "the 'talent' of the star includes striking photogenic looks, acting ability, presence on camera, charm and personality, sex appeal, attractive voice and bearing". (Jarvie, 1970)

FROM SILENT MOVIE TO TOTAL REALISM

There is, in fact, an argument that star quality was easier to achieve by leaving out, or leaving to the imagination, many realistic details of the star's actual human form. The 'typical' could then be more easily seen as the 'ideal' or 'godlike', as stars were viewed in black and white and in particular without voices during the silent era. As Alexander Walker puts it: "A 'loss of illusion' was certainly one of the first effects that the talkies had on audiences. Richard Schickel defined 'silence' as the most valuable attribute of the pre-talkie stars. 'A godhead is supposed to be inscrutable. It is not expected that he speaks directly to us. It is enough that his image be present so that we may conveniently worship it.' (Schickel and Hurlburt) Once they had dialogue on their lips, the once-silent idols suffered a serious loss of divinity. They ceased to be images in a human shape personifying the emotions through the delicately graded art of pantomime. Their voices made them as real as the audiences watching them."(Walker, 1974)

We have to remember that in the absolute beginning, the very projection of film onto a screen was 'godlike', and it was only when the audiences tired of the hyperbole of pantomime images that actual stars took the place of anonymous images with names like 'The Biograph Girl'. If the godlike extension of the star's image became more human – with the advent of voices, colour and in particular Hollywood's increasing treatment of social themes – it did not destroy the concept of the star. It merely demystified the parameters of the image in what some media academics have termed a 'bourgeois transformation'.

THE STAR AUDIENCE RELATIONSHIP

To what extent does the audience define the star, or to put it in socio-logical terms, how much is the star a phenomenon of consumption, not of production? Firstly, there are some practical facts to consider. One is that film is a medium where the consumer is predominantly female. Consequently, the male stars are both more important and more highly paid: "It is women who primarily go to the movies, women who influence men to go to the movies with them, and it's women sitting in audiences all over the world paying to see men with sex appeal on the screen. For this reason, when you cast a film an actress will be allocated 20 per cent of the casting budget, and the actor 80 per cent." (Leigh-Kile 1999) The role of the leading man in defining the film is therefore crucial, and consequently male stars even have the prerogative of making comebacks after periods of being cool in the box office. Richard Gere is a typical example – hot property after 'American Gigolo' and 'An Officer and a Gentleman', his career sunk over a number of box office flops until 'Pretty Woman' made him hot again at age forty. Women, on the other hand, seldom get a second chance, and age works heavily against them.

On a psychological level, how does the audience relate to their stars? Leo Handel found that people's favourite stars when questioned were not those of the opposite sex, which would have indicated star-audience relationships based on sexual attraction, but those of the same sex, indicating a relationship built predominantly on self-identification (Handel, 1976). Andrew Tudor (Tudor, 1974) supports this, and goes on to define four categories of star-audience relationship:

Emotional affinity. This is the most common and assumed to be "a normal sense of involvement". Tudor sees this as the weakest bond, but from a psychological perspective it would appear to be important, in that it underpins the star's charismatic attraction and the audience's motivation in "caring for" and feeling attachment towards the figures seen on the screen.

Self-identification. This is a stronger sense of involvement, according to Tudor, where the audience "places himself or herself in the same situation and persona of the star". (He cites one woman interviewee saying "These actresses I mentioned are great. They make me feel every emotion of their parts. I feel as if I were myself on the screen experiencing what they do.")

Fame

Imitation. This is assumed to be most common amongst the young, and takes the star-audience relationship outside the bounds of the cinema itself with "the star acting as some sort of model for the audience". It also opens up the whole social debate about whether the star acts as a role model for others in society, and the even more volatile psychological debate over copycat behaviour of violent or sexual material. (Eysenk and Nias, 1978)

Projection. Tudor believes that imitation turns into projection "at the point at which the process becomes more than a simple mimicking of clothing, hairstyle, kissing and the like".

Projection in the psychoanalytical sense is defined as the attribution to others of inner urges that are difficult to accept in oneself. Those who deny their own sexual urges, for instance, are likely to see others as sexually promiscuous and irresponsible and may, in watching such behaviour on film, be exploring their own unconscious desires.

But we have a paradox here: women self-identify with other women, with whom they feel emotionally involved, but the box office tells us that it is the male stars who sell films. The male/female star appeal is further complicated by factors such as the genre of film in which stars appear. According to Joe Roth, the chairman of Twentieth Century Fox, "Much of what sells big in the movie business are outsized, fantasy, action pictures and I think that men have a very difficult time going to see women in these roles. Male stars get paid more than female stars because men will go out to see men, and women will go out to see men, and men have a difficult time going out to see women. I think, quite frankly, it is sexism." (Kent, 1991)

Sexism it may be, but if both sexes prefer their action heroes to be men, then it is only realistic box office strategy for the studios to supply this. Added to this, for "a normal sense of involvement" (Tudor's terminology) to be present in the audience, the role models must be credible. Superman was bound to be more popular than Wonderwoman because heightened physical power is generally a more plausible attribute in a man (hence the Stallone and Schwarzenegger roles). But such is the film public's inherent resistance to simplistic categorisation that female action heroes – with appropriate suspension of disbelief – have also at times become cult figures, for instance Xena: Warrior Princess, or Sigourney Weaver in 'Alien' toting an automatic weapon almost as heavy as herself. One could argue, however, that in the world of science fiction anything is possible.

This added dimension of unpredictability, prejudice or bias in the audience helps supports the accepted wisdom amongst film academics that it is much harder to see the star as a phenomenon of consumption, since the parameters of consumption are both fickle and hard to quantify. "What is clear from this account (Tudor) of the star/audience relationship is that the audience's role in shaping the star phenomenon is very limited. That is, the account tells us what audiences do with the star images that they are offered and hence indicates the sources of the success of stardom, but it does not tell us why the offered images take the form they do." (Dyer, 1998) The full overview of how stars establish their reputations takes in both the fact that stars are initially chosen by the studios or cast in certain films, and it is the crucial audience response which determines which stars are 'hot' and which are not. As Alberoni put it "the star system never creates the star, but it proposes the candidate for 'election', and helps to retain the favour of the 'electors'." (Alberoni, 1972)

WHAT IS REAL – THE STAR OR THE ROLE?
Is the star fictitious or real? It is both, in different ways. Take, for instance, Rudolf Valentino – the archetypal screen lover. Was he, in reality, this person? In real life he had been a dancer and general man-about-town. On screen he was 'The Sheikh' – full of oriental exoticism and sexual mystique. In his later life he found that image hard to maintain off screen, and ironically his image might be considered indirectly to have killed him. Expected to be the great lover, he was invested with a god-like sexual potency which elevated him so high that when he had to undergo an operation no mortal surgeon was thought up to the job. Valentino was not operated on in time and died. "It was the last farce of his life – his death was a theatrical triumph. The funeral in Hollywood was one of the film world's events of the century." (James, 1993) A similarly fatal confusion between image and reality befell Houdini – expected to be able to withstand all manner of physical assault, he was punched in the stomach by a fan when he was unprepared, and died of internal injuries as a result. The ultimate confusion of media and reality happened when audiences listening to Orson Welles' radio adaptation of 'The War of the Worlds' panicked, believing

an invasion to actually have taken place, and had to be placated by announcements from the radio station that this was fictitious.

Such confusion between role and reality is well known in the world of long running TV soaps. Actors become so identified by the public with the roles they play that they can be stopped in the street and talked to as if they actually were the character, with stern advice as to what they should or should not do in the next episodes. This is an example of the public believing the character first and the person second. But it can also happen the other way around, as Griffith states in 'The Movie Stars': "The people of the movies come before us first of all as people, and only secondarily as actors – artists – if at all." (Griffith, 1970) This would be true of actors such as John Wayne and Marilyn Monroe who gave their credibility to the role and not vice versa.

But the role confusion is not only in the external world of 'life as life' or 'life as theatre'. It also exists in the heads of the audience. They see the actor in three ways. First as himself or herself – the knowable, constant and 'authentic' self. Then as the 'performing' self – how he or she acts in the presence of different people and circumstances – and finally as the 'dream' self in which the audience can fantasise about being the actor. So we have a complex interrelation between the real and fantasy selves of the audience and those of the star.

In the case of the soap star 'becoming' his or her role, for instance, it is not the authentic person of the actor that we relate to but the way the actor authenticates the part. During the soap itself the actor is predominantly the authenticated role and the audience willingly suspends its disbelief, as Plato puts it. When seated in the studio as him or herself for chat shows outside the context of the soap, the actor is mainly authentic. But even as themselves, with their real accents and life histories, such actors may be referred to by their role and are usually interrogated as to what the role person will be doing next in the script.

In a different but parallel way, musicians may become associated with their 'hits' long after they have grown artistically or simply 'moved on'. This phenomenon applies to some extent even in the classical world. Violin prodigy Nigel Kennedy is said to have stated "If anyone asks me to play the Mendelssohn Concerto again I'll punch 'em in the mouth", and has constantly experimented with his image and repertoire to avoid stagnation. But it is most true of popular music. Pop stars who developed images and even names in collective bands, like 'Ginger Spice' in the Spice Girls, have afterwards struggled for authentic identities. Crossover musicians like Chick Corea and Keith Jarrett have struggled to have their 'classical' identities recognised, though both are very fine all-round musicians and composers. Like pop singer Elvis Costello, who now performs and records with a string quartet, they have had difficulty changing an image already established in the public's mind. Actor musicians like Madonna and Frank Sinatra have been accepted more readily as that old catch phrase, the all-round entertainer, partly because the public has been conditioned to singer-actors from long exposure to opera, music hall and musical theatre. Yet role confusions still exist, some singers belonging to the Actors' Equity Union and others to the Musicians' Union.

REFERENCES

Alberoni, F (1972) The Powerless Elite, in McQuail D.(ed.) *Sociology of Mass Communications*, London, Penguin

Berne, Eric (1973) *Sex in Human Loving*, London, Penguin

Boorstin, Daniel (1963) *The Image*, London, Penguin

Caine, Hall (1882) *Recollections of Rossetti*

Dawkins, Richard (1976) *The Selfish Gene*, New York, Oxford University Press

Dyer, Richard (1998) *Stars*, London, British Film Institute Publishing

Eysenk, HJ and Nias, DKB (1978) *Sex, Violence and the Media* London, Temple Smith

Evans, Andrew (1994) *The Secrets of Musical Confidence*, London, HarperCollins

Griffith, Richard (1970) *The Movie Stars*, NY Doubleday

Handel, Leo (1976) *Hollywood Looks at its Audience: A Report of Film Audience Research*

James, Clive (1993) *Fame in the 20th Century*, London, BBC Books

James, M and Jongeward, D (1978) *Born to Win*, Signet

Jarvie, IC (1970) *Towards a Sociology of the Cinema*, London, Routledge

Kent, Nicolas (1991) *Naked Hollywood*, London, BBC Books

Leigh-Kile, Donna (1999) *Sex Symbols*, London, Vision Paperbacks.

Fame

Morin, Edgar (1960) *The Stars*, NY, Grove Press

Powdermaker, Hortense (1950) *The Dream Factory*, Boston, Little Brown

Shipman, David (1991) *The Great Movie Stars* Vols. 1–3, London, Warner Books

Celebrities, NTC Business Books

Tudor, Andrew (1974) *Image and Influence, Studies in the Sociology of Film* London, Allen and Unwin

Walker, Alexander (1974) *Stardom*, London, Penguin

FACTORS IN FAME

S ome are born famous. Some work hard to achieve fame. Others have fame thrust upon them. This is a terse summary of the main sources of fame. Some are famous simply because of who they are (as with most monarchs, an accident of birth). Some set out with the averred intention of becoming famous, and scheme and plot their way to the top (such as marrying a film producer). They may seem to work hard to achieve what they do, but might have been extremely ruthless along the path. Some have extraordinary looks or personal characteristics that cannot fail to get them noticed, and others become famous as a by-product of making some contribution to art, science, literature, humanity, or some other area of human endeavour. For such people, who may be shy and introvert by nature, fame can be an embarrassment or seem like an invasion of their privacy. Einstein could never quite acclimatise to the fact that people were interested in him as a person as much as his theories.

Sheer familiarity may be sufficient to engender fame (as in the case of those who read weather reports on TV). The perpetration of a single ghastly deed or series of crimes will produce notoriety, which is a particular form of fame. Finally, the public may take to their heart some fairly nondescript individual and project a fantasy upon them (cf 'The Life Of Brian', the Monty Python film in which a very ordinary man is identified as the Messiah by a gullible crowd looking for anybody to lead and inspire them). What follows is a closer look at some of the factors that contribute to the acquisition of fame.

LETTING IT ALL HANG OUT

Of all the personality traits that make for fame, a degree of exhibitionism would seem to be most important. This is particularly obvious in those who have achieved fame merely by streaking (running nude) through a well-televised arena such as a football pitch or a royal wedding. A few years ago, a hitherto unknown young woman called Erica Roe attracted massive media attention and appeared on several TV chat shows following such a (supposedly spontaneous) gesture at a Twickenham rugby international. An exhibitionist element is equally apparent in those who have achieved celebrity by posing nude in wide circulation newspapers or magazines. Marilyn Monroe first sprang to popular attention when she posed nude for a 'Playboy' calendar, while Samantha Fox and Melinda Messenger went from being Page 3 Girls in

Fame

tabloid newspapers to TV presenter roles.

In recent years, we have witnessed an enormous increase in the number of chat shows and fly-on-the-wall documentaries in which ordinary members of the public seek their statutory fifteen minutes of fame by exposing their sins and weaknesses to an ever more voyeuristic public. 'The Jerry Springer Show', with its motto 'no subject too indecent, no individual too pathetic', is perhaps the apotheosis of this genre, but there are many close runners. These programmes have so-called researchers who are commissioned to seek out grotesque people with bizarre stories, who are prepared to reveal all on the screen. Sometimes they are paid a small amount, described as expenses, but in any case, they are usually delighted to appear just for a taste of fame. Such is the desire for fame among some of these studio guests that they do not care how ridiculous they seem; some will even risk arrest by describing illegal activities such as paedophile sexual contacts on screen. Others invent stories and describe outrageous behaviour that they know will get them onto the screen.

TV companies have not usually cared too much whether these people, or their stories, are genuine. Only recently, after a British documentary about a father and daughter had to be dropped at great expense because it was discovered that it actually featured a girl and her older boyfriend (the father having refused to co-operate) have TV companies shown much concern about being duped. Shortly afterwards, some producers were fired from the 'Vanessa' show, when it was discovered that they were using agency actors to play normal people enmeshed in love tangles of one sort or another. What comes out of these various phenomena is the impression that exhibitionism, especially in the service of fame acquisition, is widespread.

Even in orthodox avenues of performance, such as acting, singing, dancing and conjuring, an impulse to seek attention and show off seems to be involved. Putting oneself before a public, whether on stage or TV camera, or making a political speech, implies a need for recognition, a kind of adult equivalent of the child's cry of 'Mummy, Daddy, look at me' before leaping into a swimming pool. This desire to be watched and applauded often needs to be strong enough to combat and override almost equally powerful fears of public failure and humiliation that are experienced as stage fright. Without this fundamental drive to stand up in front of people and do a turn, many people who are recognised as celebrities would surely have remained in obscurity. The conclusion that performers, as a group, are high on personality traits variously labelled 'exhibitionism', 'expressiveness' and 'extraversion' is confirmed by research using standard personality tests (Wilson, 1994).

Accepting that an exhibitionistic streak often helps in becoming famous, from whence does this trait arise? A popular psychoanalytic theory is that attention-seeking behaviour in adulthood stems from insufficient parental attention at a formative phase of childhood development. Deprived of love at some critical time in babyhood the individual is stuck in a groove of neurotic 'neediness' for attention that pushes them to the permanent pursuit of praise and applause. Dustin Hoffman may serve as an illustration. He was skinny and tiny as a child, wore teeth braces for eight years, and had an older brother who was clever and good at sport, to whom he felt inferior. He was frequently taunted by other children who told him his nose was big and his darting eyes made him look like a rat. His own interpretation was that he became an actor in order to cope with these childhood problems and gain some much needed recognition (Bates, 1986). This, of course, is similar to the Adlerian idea that small men often strive to offset their diminutive stature with a lust for extraordinary power (cf Napoleon, Hitler and Mussolini).

This 'compensation' theory is appealing, but it lacks scientific verification. It is just as easy to find examples of people who were starved of parental attention and who grew up to be engineers or accountants. To make matters worse, the behaviourists and social learning theorists have floated an opposing but equally plausible idea. Psychologists of these persuasions argue that exhibitionism, as a personality trait, arises from a history of reinforcement for outgoing and theatrical forms of behaviour dating from early childhood. In other words, some children learn from an early age that their parents reward them for performing their party piece, with the result that expressive behaviour becomes magnified and habitual. Shirley Temple might be cited as a case in point; having gained a taste for stardom as a child actress, when her performing career faltered she went on to develop a career in politics (an equally high-profile occupation).

As this 'reinforcement' theory is virtually the reverse of the deprivation idea, which is correct? There may be some element of truth to each. Perhaps they apply in individual cases, such as the examples given above, to an approximately even degree (such that they cancel each other out across the board and cannot be detected by scientific data gatherers). On the other hand, there is reason to believe that both theories are largely wrong. Modern behaviour genetics has developed statistical techniques (based on twin and family relationship data) for determining how much of the variation on a particular trait is due to heredity, how much is due to the shared family environment, and how much is due to non-shared family environmental factors. Both the above theories presume that the shared family environment (things experienced jointly with other members of the same family, such as religious values or permissive attitudes) would be of key importance. However, the research evidence suggests that this source of variation contributes virtually nothing to personality. Instead, personality traits like extraversion (which includes aspects of exhibitionism) seem to be determined about half by heredity and half by environmental factors that are not shared by other family members (Loehlin, 1992).

Putting this another way, insofar as our personality resembles that of our parents and siblings it is for genetic reasons, not the way we have been raised. Of course, this leaves room for interactive effects, such as our looks determining the way others react to us, or perceiving our parents as treating our siblings more favourably than ourselves, to be important in building our character. Indeed, sibling rivalry could well be influential because it falls within the realm of non-shared environment (a force promoting personality differences within the same family). Hence while we can be fairly certain that exhibitionism as a personality characteristic does relate to fame, we can be less sure of the origins of this trait. Partly, it is constitutional and partly it is determined by unknown environmental influences, including physical effects such as drugs our mother may have taken during pregnancy, forceps delivery or infantile meningitis. What doesn't seem to count for very much (surprisingly) is the way that our parents treat us. Indeed, the way our parents behave towards us may be largely a result of the kind of person we are and the way in which we behave towards them.

CHARMING THE PANTS OFF
Being a show-off is all very well but it is equally important to have

something worth looking at. Personal charm is an attribute that promotes fame, and this is sometimes called charisma. Charisma refers to 'the power of presence' – a certain magnetism or magic that is generated when an individual appears on a stage or merely walks into a room. To some extent this depends upon physical attributes such as beauty (Claudia Schiffer, Ingrid Bergman), sexual attractiveness (Marilyn Monroe), physical stature (Arnold Schwarzenegger), skill (Tiger Woods), assertiveness (Humphrey Bogart), quality of voice (Elvis Presley, Pavarotti), or some mixture of these commodities (John Wayne, Sean Connery, Laurence Olivier). But fame leads to charisma even more surely than charisma leads to fame, so that fairly ordinary looking people (Prince Charles, Henry Kissinger, Woody Allen, Albert Einstein) can electrify a social situation because of who they are (their institutional status) or what they have achieved. Other people acquire charisma because they are interesting or amusing (Robin Williams; Jim Carrey). Even simple exposure (familiarity) may lend charisma, as with TV newsreaders, weather reporters and game-show bimbos. Distinctive deficiencies (Oliver Hardy's plumpness, Danny DeVito's shortness, Yul Brynner's baldness) may make an individual more memorable, and hence more famous. The ideal charismatic combination is, however, a combination of looks, positive personality features and social position (John F. Kennedy; Diana, Princess of Wales). Given such a package, media attention follows almost inevitably.

We may find charismatic individuals likeable (Muhammad Ali, Mikhail Gorbachev, Benny Hill) but this is not a necessary virtue. People who appear as cold, surly and abrasive (Margaret Thatcher, Clint Eastwood, James Dean) may also be charismatic – even outright villains (Adolf Hitler, Saddam Hussein). A number of women find they cannot resist a loveable rogue such as Errol Flynn or Bill Clinton. The reason seems to be that we have a sneaking regard for people who are independent of thought and action (following their own drums) even if this is taken to an anti-social degree. As Bates (1986) points out, self-assurance is a key element of charisma, and this can be defined as 'the strength to resist the need to be liked'. People who are uncompromising in being themselves exude a kind of power that contributes to charisma. Such an attribute is especially important to politicians, for whom looks, voice and self-confident body language count for much more than any message they might seek to convey (Lanone and

Fame

Schrott, 1989). In addition, it appears that many women are attracted to arrogant and ruthless men because of the hypermasculine buzz that they emit, an attraction that may prove fatal when they attach themselves to wife-beaters like OJ Simpson.

While films and TV shows may feature great actors and actresses such as Alec Guinness, Peter Sellers and Robert De Niro who assume a variety of different characters, the true 'stars' are those who always play themselves. Thus James Stewart, John Wayne, James Dean and Marilyn Monroe made little attempt to alter their portrayals from one appearance to the next; their own personalities were sufficiently charismatic to ensure a following. The idolisation received by such personality stars goes beyond mere admiration and seems to reflect some deep-seated need within the public. It seems we have a desire to crystallise certain feelings and preoccupations (relating to sexuality, power, freedom amongst others) by personifying them. Marilyn Monroe was the epitome of female desirability (blonde, voluptuous and vulnerable), John Wayne represented the no-nonsense tough guy, and James Dean typified moody rebellious youth. These stereotypes became stamped upon the performer to the extent that they were expected by the public to conform to them consistently, both upon the screen and in real life. "Chosen to enact our dreams, they must make themselves over to us utterly, resigning tenure of their own existence." (Conrad, 1987) Particularly if they die young, such superstars become immortal, with anniversaries being celebrated, relics exchanged, conspiracy theories advanced and various attempts made at resurrection (eg the 'Elvis is alive' campaign). Celebrity status, then, is determined not just by the objective characteristics of the individual but also by the way in which the population at large adopts them as an incarnation of their fantasies.

WHAT'S IN A NAME?

In early (silent) films the stars were often not named because studios feared that they might become so popular that they would demand higher fees. Later they realised that the 'star cult', while increasing their wages bill, would ultimately pay off by increasing interest in the film. Then it became important to have the right name, so that many of the stars that were put under contract adopted a name chosen for them by the studio.

Some names were changed because they were intrinsically unattractive. Frances Gumm became Judy Garland. Harry Webb became Cliff Richard. Diana Fluck became Diana Dors. Reginald Dwight became Elton John. Archie Leach (the name adopted by John Cleese in 'A Fish Called Wanda' because it sounds slightly ridiculous) was the original name of Cary Grant. Even without knowing the characters attached to them, the latter name has a more confident, masculine clipped-consonant sound about it, like Clark Gable or Kirk Douglas. Marilyn Monroe was originally Norma Jean Baker, and it is probably no coincidence that her adopted name has female, 'mammary' overtones. Psycholinguists point out virtually all cultures use a word like mama or mummy to represent mother and this derives from the closed-lip infant sucking motion. 'M' is a very, comforting, feminine consonant (humming and the mantra 'om' are inclined to be relaxing). It is, therefore, obvious why John Wayne could hardly have made it as a hard-hitting cowboy star under his original name of Marion Morrison!

When Laurence Olivier first broke into Hollywood films the studio bosses thought his name sounded too foreign and would be difficult to pronounce and remember. He therefore came under pressure to change it to Larry Oliver, which sensibly he resisted, particularly in view of the distinguished Shakespearean roles that followed. The studios were right to believe that a name should be memorable, but they failed to realise that a complex and unusual name, once remembered, is harder to forget. Guiseppe Verdi may be harder for Anglo-Americans to acquire than Joe Green, but it sticks better in the memory.

Another well established principle in judgements of fame is that of prior exposure (Carroll and Buss, 1988). If people have heard a name before (or even its components separately) they are more likely to attribute fame to its owner. A good example is the singer Engelbert Humperdinck, who blatantly stole the name of a famous Victorian German composer, presumably to avail himself of the familiarity effect. The name was no doubt bobbing about in the subconscious of many people who, not being opera buffs, would have recognised the name without being able to identify it as the composer of 'Hansel and Gretel'. It certainly appeared to work because "Engelbert" had been around for some time under the name of Gerry Dorsey without gaining much attention. Tom Jones did not change his name but he may have been fortunate in sharing the name with the character in Fielding's novel, which became a very popular film starring Albert Finney around the time Tom was establishing his career. Another British singer who gained popularity in the 1980s adopted the name Rose Marie, and may thus have benefited from the earlier fame of Sigmund Romberg's operetta. Actress Joyce Frankenberg changed her name to Jane Seymour, thus benefiting from reminiscence of Henry VIII's wife of the same name.

Muhammad Ali was the name adopted by Cassius Clay to announce his conversion to Islam in typically grandiose fashion, and this decision in itself caused great media excitement at the time. Perhaps the most intriguing (if gimmicky) exercise in making a name noticeable was that undertaken by Prince. Besides escaping a binding music contract, he helped to revive press interest in his career by renaming himself with an abstract, unpronounceable symbol and requiring journalists and presenters to describe him as The Artist Formerly Known as Prince.

Of course, in none of these instances would the name alone have been sufficient to account for the career success of the individual. It does seem certain, however, that having a name that is distinctive and which conjures appropriate images (macho, sexy or romantic), or which arouses emotions of any kind (for example Judas Priest, Sid Vicious) can be advantageous to a career.

IF AT FIRST YOU DON'T SUCCEED…

Motivation is also a key factor in achieving fame. Drive, determination, persistence, single-mindedness, ambition (call it what you will), can make all the difference between triumph and obscurity. The singer Madonna is a good example. She was one of eight children of a car plant worker in Detroit, nice-looking but not exceptionally so, and perhaps only moderately talented as a singer, dancer and actress, yet she rose to world fame as an entertainer and an $80 million dollar fortune. Why? According to Burchill (1992), "strength" is the answer. "In a landscape of wimps, she is a force of nature, like a hurricane, with so much faith in herself that, sometimes, she appears to be on the verge of the psychotic." Martin Amis (1992) refers to her "flair for manipulation…her innate amorality her talent for ruthlessness…Madonna's protean quality, her ability to redesign herself (evident in each new photo-shoot: baby-doll, dominatrix, flower-child, vamp) represents an emphasis of will over talent. Not greatly gifted, not deeply beautiful, Madonna tells America that fame comes from wanting it badly enough."

It is easy to forget that Marilyn Monroe was not always a star, and had to fight very hard for recognition. Norman Mailer (1973) recounts that, as a starlet, she had great difficulty in attracting the eye of studio boss Darryl Zanuck, so she concentrated on posing for publicity stills that found their way to national newspapers. Deciding to be dramatic one day when called for a photo shoot, she changed into a semi-transparent gown in wardrobe and walked the six blocks to the gallery. "Barefooted, her long hair streaming loosely behind her, her skin clearly visible under the diaphanous negligee, she floated along the studio streets." The news quickly spread and by the time she started back the streets were lined with cheering studio employees. Items about the escapade appeared in the trade press and Marilyn was the talk of Hollywood. When, shortly afterwards, she appeared (late as usual) at a studio publicity party 20th Century Fox's leading stars were "trampled to death in the stampede for Marilyn".

This capacity to be calculating in the furtherance of one's ambitions has been called Machiavellianism by psychologists (after the recipes for acquiring and maintaining political power outlined by the medieval sociologist Machiavelli in his book 'The Prince'). Questionnaires to assess this as a personality trait have been devised (Christie and Geis, 1970), high 'Mach' scorers being described as practical, cynical, expedient, unsentimental and manipulative in their dealings with others. This, in turn, is related to various other traits such as 'tough-mindedness', 'achievement motivation' and 'the Protestant work-ethic', all of which point up the importance of detachment, hard graft, and 'stickability' in career progress. Centuries before Edison's oft-quoted remark about genius being "1% inspiration and 99% perspiration", an (unnamed) ancient Greek poet wrote "before the gates of excellence the Gods have placed sweat".

However, keeping your nose to the grindstone in a rather pedestrian pursuit is one of the last ways of achieving greatness. Some element of 'vision' usually has to be added, together with a degree of devotion to it that is likely to be seen by others as cranky. The composer Richard Wagner worked on his 'Ring Cycle' for some 30 years before completion and then insisted that it could not be performed before a new custom-built theatre (Bayreuth) was available. Even by Wagner's own eccentric standards this project was regarded as so ambitious that his sponsor King Ludwig (who was himself somewhat grandiose) thought he had taken leave of his senses. Today, however, this four-part opera series is widely hailed as one of the greatest artistic achievements of all time. Charles Darwin (although considered a failure in early life, being unable to complete studies in medicine or the ministry) began to formulate his ideas about evolution in the early 1830s. Aware of the resistance he was bound to encounter, he proceeded to gather data and refine his theories of another 20 years before astounding the world with his 'Origin of Species'. The great innovators throughout history have tended to mix original insights with a perseverance and zeal amounting to fanaticism.

The motivational factor may account for two other observations. One is the fact that outstanding advances, particularly in art and science, are usually made by people who are highly productive (Simonton, 1997). In other words, there is a correlation between the quantity and quality of people's creative output; those who produce the most frequently produce the best (WA Mozart and Sir Francis Galton). The other (more controversial) observation concerns the preponderance of males over females as regards the acquisition of fame in many fields such as science and technology, art and musical composition, politics and business enterprise (Wilson, 1989). When The Sunday Times (28/3/99) published a list of the 50 top masterpieces of the millennium, only one ('Pride and Prejudice') was contributed by a woman. This may partly be due to differences in ability and opportunity, but the main factor is probably the intense competitiveness and perseverance of men in these fields. Women tend to regard other things such as love and family as supremely important and are less inclined to sacrifice these values for their work. Some, such as Anita Roddick and Nicola Horlick, have managed to combine business success with raising a family, but it is not by coincidence that women most frequently achieve distinction in people-oriented fields of endeavour such as novel-writing (Jane Austen and the Bronte sisters) and humanitarianism (Florence Nightingale, Mother Teresa).

Factors in Fame

A LUST FOR LIFE (OR LIFE OF LUST?)

The casual observer could hardly fail to be impressed by the complex love lives lived by so many famous people. This could be partly because the media is interested in the sex lives of the famous more than those of ordinary people, so that the philandering of a John F Kennedy or a Bill Clinton makes news whereas the dirty deeds of the rest of us are studiously ignored. It is also possible that some people in the limelight, especially Hollywood stars, deliberately complicate their own sex lives because it generates publicity (and, as publicist Max Clifford might attest, "there is no such thing as bad publicity"). But beyond these selective effects, it does appear that a rampant libido is one manifestation of a generalised drive toward experiencing life fully, which helps to elevate people to the top levels of their chosen career. Hence creativity, achievement and sex drive are linked phenomena.

The male sex hormone testosterone may have a role in this connection. Testosterone not only increases libido (of the predatory, rather than loving, variety) but it also promotes competitiveness and creativity. Constructions such as the Taj Mahal, Wagner's 'Ring Cycle' and Bertrand Russell's 'Principia Mathematica' may be parallel in some sense to the courtship motivated industry of the bower bird (a New Guinea species in which the males build elaborate coloured gardens and towers to attract females to their territory, rather than drag heavy plumage around on their own tails like the peacock), or the singing of canaries (which also depends upon male sex hormones). Gifted and successful men, in any field, do attract more females; having more wives, mistresses, children (and divorces) than less productive men. The two men mentioned above are good examples. Wagner managed to love other men's wives as well as his own (sometimes with the connivance, or at least grudging acceptance, of their husbands), and Bertrand Russell was married four times. Charlie Chaplin, another much-married man noted for creative output, once said "every man, whether he be young or old, when meeting any woman, measures the potentiality of sex between them. Thus it has always been with me." He may have been talking for himself but one suspects that much the same would apply to many Hollywood stars through the years, such as Errol Flynn, Warren Beatty, Michael Douglas, and David Duchovny. (The latter two have supposedly admitted to obsessional levels of libido and sought treatment for "sex addiction"). Nor is this connection necessarily limited to men; certain women, from Cleopatra to Madonna, have combined great achievement with sexual adventurousness. In the case of some, such as Katherine the Great of Russia and Lillie Langtry, sexual exploits contribute a major part of their fame.

Studies of testosterone levels in people of different occupations confirm the relationship between libido and social prominence. Actors and sportspeople (two groups for whom fame comes readily) have higher testosterone levels than ministers of religion and salesmen (Dabbs, et al, 1990). Women, on the other hand, who compete in male dominated fields such as business and politics have higher testosterone levels than those who maintain a domestic lifestyle (Purifoy and Koopmans, 1979). But, of course, testosterone levels are responsive to the experience of social dominance as well as contributing to it, so this relationship is almost bound to appear. For example, the winner of a sports contest like a boxing match or Wimbledon Final shows an increase in testosterone following his victory while the defeated one shows a decline, and the same applies to women. Therefore, the more significant effects of testosterone consist in the pre-priming of neural circuits before birth, which simultaneously lay the foundations for competitive and sexually adventurous behaviour.

It is not necessary to be a heterosexual male in order to be the beneficiary of the energising effects of testosterone. As noted, testosterone increases the competitiveness and predatory sexual behaviour of women as well. Homosexual men throughout history have also made remarkable contributions to art, politics and other fields, and have achieved great fame. One thinks of Socrates, Michelangelo, Tchaikovsky, Oscar Wilde, Noel Coward, Cole Porter, Leonard Bernstein, Benjamin Britten, not to mention numerous actors and pop musicians. It is possible that homosexual men have an advantage in that they have all the drive of a typical male without incurring family responsibilities to the same extent. Many top female athletes are lesbian in orientation as well as some of the greatest female achievers (for example novelist Virginia Woolf and Dame Ethel Smythe, arguably the greatest ever female composer.)

YOU DON'T HAVE TO BE MAD – BUT IT MAY HELP!
Another broad trait of personality relevant to the acquisition of power

and fame is that which psychologists call psychoticism. This combines elements of bizarre and original thinking (sometimes called 'schizo-typy') with grandiose ('manic') schemes and often an anti-social (perhaps even 'psychopathic') determination to see them carried through. Eysenck (1995) reviews evidence that genius derives partly from a tendency to psychoticism, both being associated with an excess of a neurotransmitter called dopamine and a deficit of another called serotonin. Moderate levels of psychoticism seem to broaden perceptual and associative horizons (producing 'overinclusive thinking') and this promotes the discovery of remote associations, a basis of creative inspiration. Of course, other factors such as high intelligence, confidence in ones own ideas and persistence (as mentioned above) are also important to the manifestation of genius, but psychoticism may be the real key to creative genius. The stereotype of the 'mad scientist' is widely recognised, as is the fact that many great artists and composers were of dubious sanity.

One of the best examples is the Spanish painter Salvador Dali. According to his biographer (Gibson, 1996), Dali resolved to be flamboyant and outrageous from an early age. "I'll be a genius – they will admire me" he wrote at age 16. His determination to shock was helped by an apparent absence of scruples or empathy. He liked throwing cats into swimming pools and once planned to blow up some live swans by feeding them explosives. He was naturally attracted to fascism, was contemptuous of ordinary people, whom he referred to as "the normal putrid pig", and claimed that the aim of his art was to "cretinise the public". Female sexuality filled him with loathing and he could not bear to be touched; his sole outlet was masturbation, which he organised as group recreation. He bought a castle for his nymphomaniac wife Gala to entertain her numerous toyboys. As she grew older, however, fighting decay with facelifts and live-cell injections, he could not bear to see her and spent the last seven years of his life lying alone in the dark being force fed with a plastic tube in his nose. His surrealistic art, filled with symbols such as swastikas, rotting donkeys, drooping clocks and fishheads, seems to echo his cold and delusional life. Although capable of painting with great technical skill (clearly apparent in his early works), he was devoid of artistic integrity and around 1965 began signing blank sheets of paper at the rate of 1000 per hour, which he sold for $10 each. Was he a genius or a madman? Probably a bit of both, and the same may be said of many other great artists, such as William Blake, Van Gogh, Picasso and Gaugin.

Many of the world's greatest composers also had mental problems, most commonly affective disorders, including manic-depressive psychosis. Schumann, Handel, Berlioz and Rachmaninoff suffered major mood swings. Gluck, Beethoven and Wolf had psychotic tendencies whilst Bach, Liszt, Mahler, Schubert, J. Strauss (Jnr) and Wagner are considered by some to have been psychopathic. Berg, Berlioz, Bruckner, Elgar, Gounod, Moussorgsky, Puccini, Scriabin and Tchaikovsky displayed various forms of neurosis such as depression or obsessionality, and Mozart may have had Tourette's Syndrome (uncontrollable tics and obscenities). While some of these attributions may be arguable, it does appear that up to half of the most famous names in music suffered severe psychopathology (Frosch, 1987).

Other studies have estimated that the incidence of psychotic illness in poets, playwrights and scientists (among other creative occupations) is at least three times that of the population at large, and this applies particularly to those who are most eminent (Jamison, 1989; Post, 1994). Again, bipolar (manic-depressive) psychosis is particularly common, with high productivity most often appearing in the manic, rather than depressive, phase of the illness. For such people the 'flight of ideas' that they experience during the manic episode is a rich vein for their creativity to tap.

When Ionesco wrote his first play, 'The Bald Primadonna', he hesitated to have it staged, fearing that it exposed his own madness; he was both relieved and delighted to discover that audiences found it funny. Dennis Potter achieved fame as a TV playwright with series such as 'Pennies from Heaven' and 'The Singing Detective' because he was able to turn his personal fantasies and obsessions (particularly his insecurity and disgust with sex) into entertainment. WS Gilbert (of Gilbert and Sullivan fame) was also abnormal in personality, being authoritarian, boastful and vindictive. He was obsessed with murder, executions and torture and with large, ageing and sexually threatening women, both in his poetry and drama and in real life. Biographer David Eden (1986) offers a Freudian interpretation of Gilbert's preoccupations, tracing them to infantile sadomasochism (fixation at the emotional level of a 5 year old child). He also presents evidence that Gilbert, although married, was probably impotent throughout life. Such writers seem to draw on their own psychopathology to generate literary material.

Many performers also suffer from (or derive creative energy from) mental disturbances. Top pianists such as Glenn Gould, Claudio Arrau and John Ogden come readily to mind, as do some of the world's greatest comedians. Peter Sellers was "certifiable" according to producer Blake Edwards. He was insanely superstitious; he had to sleep facing north, consulted spiritualists and astrologers for career advice, and could not abide the colour green in his presence. He once demanded that the Hotel Crillon brick off a bathroom because it was duck-egg blue, had a whole train repainted during filming of 'The Prisoner of Zenda' and objected to the green baize in a casino scene (Lewis, 1994). Added to this was a tendency for bullying and cruelty (he loved to make people cry) and a "manic dissatisfaction" causing him to buy new cars and stereo equipment every few months, and relentlessly pursue famous women who were out of his reach (Sophia Loren and Princess Margaret).

Clearly, there is a link between psychosis and creativity, but it is a complex one. There are the unconventional thought patterns that schizophrenic tendencies (as well as dopamine boosting drugs such as cocaine, and even nicotine and alcohol) may inspire. There are the intense bursts of energy produced by manic illness, combined with grandiose plans and high self-evaluation. It is also possible that traumatic life experiences (such as Dennis Potter's tormented childhood or Tchaikovsky's struggle with his homosexual nature) can produce mental instability while at the same time providing emotional material that emerges in the form of art and literature. Creativity and madness seem to be genetically; psychotic people not only have more relatives who are psychotic but also more relatives who display genius. The reverse is also true. (Eysenck, 1995).

But although there are similarities between creativity and madness there are probably also some important differences. To be creative a person needs to make some contact with reality at some level or at some time; they cannot be totally lost in a fantasy world. Consider the comparison between the novelist James Joyce and his daughter Lucia who was being treated for schizophrenia by CG Jung. Joyce doubted that she could be schizophrenic because her thought patterns seemed so similar to his own. Jung disagreed, comparing father and daughter to two people who had arrived at the bottom of a river. According to Jung, James Joyce had dived there, whereas Lucia had fallen in.

REFERENCES

Amis, M (1992) Review of *Madonna's Sex* in the Observer (Magazine).

Bates, BC (1986) *The Way of the Actor*. London: Century Hutchinson.

Burchill, J (1992) *Sex and Sensibility*. London: Grafton.

Carroll, M and Buss, R (1988) *Fame attributions and the feeling of knowing*. Australian Journal of Psychology, 40, 35–43.

Christie, R and Geis, FL (1970) *Studies in Machiavellianism*. New York: Academic Press.

Conrad, P (1987) *A Song of Death: The Meaning of Opera*. London: Chatto and Windus.

Dabbs, JM, de la Rue D, and William, P.M. (1990) *Testosterone and occupational choice: Actors, ministers and other men*. Journal of Personality and Social Psychology. 59, 1261–1265.

Eysenck, HJ (1995) Genius: *The Natural History of Creativity*. Cambridge: Cambridge University Press.

Frosch, WA (1987) *Moods, madness and music: Major affective disease and musical creativity*.

Gibson, I (1996) *The Shameful Life of Salvador Dali*. London: Faber.

Jamison, K (1989) *Mood disorders and seasonal patterns in British writers and artists*. Psychiatry, 52, 125–134.

Lanone, DJ and Schrott, PR (1989) *Voters reactions to televised presidential debates: measurement of the source and magnitude of opinion change*. Political Psychology, 10, 275–285.

Lewis, R (1994) *The Life and Death of Peter Sellers*. New York: Century.

Loehlin, JC (1992) *Genes and Environment in Personality Development*. Newbury Park, CA: Sage.

Mailer, N (1973) *Marilyn*. London: Hodder and Stoughton.

Pos, F (1994) *Creativity and psychopathology*. British Journal of Psychiatry, 165, 22–34.

Purifoy, FE and Koopmans, LH (1979) *Androstenedione, testosterone, and free testosterone concentrations in women of various occupations*. Social Biology, 26, 179–188.

Simonton, DK (1997) *Genius and Creativity*. Greenwich, CT: Ablex.

Wilson, GD (1989) *The Great Sex Divide*. London: Peter Owen.

Wilson, GD (1994) *Psychology for Performing Artists: Butterflies and Bouquets*. London: Jessica Kingsley.

Fame

BECOMING FAMOUS

The pinnacle of any career is fame. Or is it? Picasso is reputed to have said that of all the unpleasant things he had known in life – poverty, disapproval, unhappiness – fame was not only the worst but worse than all the other things put together.

Why does the transition from normality into fame cause conflict? For a start, fame has a notorious way of exposing potential weaknesses and opening cracks. If there are any conflicts in motivation fame exposes them: people with ordinary lives strive to be good at what they do, but have the reassurance that they are not expected to be extraordinary. Famous people may wonder, as we all do, if they are either really that good, or really that bad. However they have the added pressure, when they face each new day, of having an image to live up to. Fame signals reaching the highest plateau of the profession, and from the top the only journey left is either straight ahead or down. The descent can be slow, or in some cases quite sudden, and may be assisted by the envy of others. As Yul Brynner observed, "They like you until you're standing on a pedestal and they hand you an Oscar. Then they say 'How did he get up there? Let's knock him down.'"

KEEPING YOUR FEET ON THE GROUND – STAGGERING LIFE CHANGES

Fame may open new and sometimes exciting doors. But as one door opens, another tends to shut. Old friends drop away or are embarrassed to make contact, and relationships break up under the stress of conflicting lifestyles. People can suddenly be stranded with a completely new framework in which to live. At times, all references are new: new management, new fellow actors or musicians, new relationship, new friends, new bank balance, new house, new country, new tour. Add to that the 'new' look in people's faces as they look straight at the 'familiar self' of the famous (the one they themselves see in the mirror in the morning) and see someone else – a 'star' with a public image. "There's a euphoria that comes with it," singer Rosemary Clooney said, "where you're not prepared for that kind of lifestyle, the unending escalation of earnings, people that you meet that you had no idea in the world you would ever associate with at all. And you're really not prepared for all of it happening so quickly. It's hard, very hard." (Boller and Davis, 1987)

Fame

The most basic advice in the face of this transition is to maintain the love of your close friends and family and keep your feet on the ground, which is how one famous actor put it. To avoid fame going to one's head, it is important to retain something of the familiar, since change in itself can be a stressor. Furthermore, multiple changes have a cumulative stress effect. A table compiled by Holmes and Rahe suggests a scale of values for common life events. The changes that frequently apply to overnight fame are given below: {INS FG.7.1}

Life event	Life change value
Marital separation	65
Business re-adjustment	39
Change in financial state	38
Change to different line of work	36
Change in responsibilities at work	29
Outstanding personal achievement	28
Change in living conditions	25
Revision of personal habits	24
Change in residence	20
Change in social activities	18
	Total = 322

Table: Holmes TH and Rahe RH (1967)

To provide a measurement of stress effects, these life changes were related to physical illness. When the total reached between 200 and 300 over a period of a year, more than half the people involved were found to show health problems the following year. For a total of over 300, the figure rose to about three-quarters. Admittedly, the subjects tested were not particularly famous and some of the factors tend to overlap, but this scale does give an indication of how a number of sudden changes in basic living values can cause a stressful readjustment when they all come at once.

Whilst change may be inevitable with the onset of fame, it is important to stagger the rate and scale of that change in order to protect against disorientation. Maintaining certain factors in ones life – crucially the people that you know and love – can allow for experimentation in other areas. Musicians have deliberately counteracted change by keeping their original bands together as much as possible and experimenting with new material – examples being The Rolling Stones and the Beatles. However, the reverse can also be true when making it to the big time enables them to work with fellow musicians they may only have dreamed about before.

TAKING CARE OF THE BUSINESS SIDE OF THINGS

Fame can further distort familiar realities when personal matters such as artistic direction, finances, image, clothes, professional direction and appointments diary are put into the hands of others. These managers, agents, accountants and other industry personnel are paid by the star to make decisions in the best interests of the star. But since they are in the industry for their own profit and success, the best interests of the star may conflict with their own best interests. It is rare for the transition to fame to occur without a considerable change in finances. Big sums of money change hands around famous people, and money can easily be lost as well as gained – there are plenty of people in the fame industry who are specifically there to take a cut of the spoils for their services. The newly created star is a commodity with value, and other people will want a piece of that value.

The advice regularly given by those who have experienced fame is to be practical, question everything, read contracts and seek help from one's union wherever appropriate. Find out about the basics, unlike the pop stars who did not know the difference between gross and net. Get a good lawyer and a good accountant, not just someone you know casually or someone recommended to you but one who can be vouched for by a number of people you trust. Do as much as you can yourself – you can trust yourself more than anyone. When asked what he would change if he had to do it all over again, Chuck Berry (who now runs all his own bookings) gave his now famous reply, "I'd do a business degree first then become a musician".

ARE SOME PERSONALITIES 'BETTER' AT FAME THAN OTHERS?

The artistic personality as a whole, as it applies to actors, musicians, writers, painters and other performers and creative people, is heavily biased towards the imaginative. This would also be true for inventors and scientists. The tendency to rely on fantasy may account for the difficulty that some famous people from these backgrounds experience in establishing realistic and objective goals for their careers, and in being practical in a general sense. There may be a concentration on the grand plan to the detriment of details, some of them important. The opposite is true of most sportspeople, who live in the present and are much more aware of actual quality of life, rather than fantasy.

Many creative people also have a distinct 'feeling', or instinctual, preference rather than a coldly analytical brain. This is frequently seen in the world of music – which is a non-analytic, non-verbal form of communication – and even more so in the world of art. It is also reflected in a strong bias towards helping and caring, shown in the kind of charity work for which the showbiz world is legendary, and indeed in self-help through various methods. Musicians and other 'feeling' people tend as a whole to have warm personalities and to value the fellowship that is found in the profession. The drawbacks for such people include a dependency on praise, and a sensitivity to being criticised. They are vulnerable to being ignored or misunderstood – even by people who are not capable of understanding them artistically, by people with suspect financial motives, or by critics who may not give a fair comment. 'Feeling' people may continually look for acceptance from those who show a consistent inability to provide it, and this can and often does lead to depression. The opposite is true of politicians, who tend to be rational, analytic and more concerned with principles than people, and are more offended by injustice than hurt by indifference.

Another problem with the 'feeling' preference is the desire to be 'nice' to people. This is particularly inappropriate with financial matters. One should either practise being tougher or reserve 'another part of the brain' for dealing coldly and efficiently with business matters. This is sometimes a hard lesson to learn (and one frequently learned with the hindsight of experience) because it goes 'against one's personality type'. The very artistic gifts and essential charisma that characterises some famous people can be antithetical to the business world in which they have to live and survive, which helps to explain why some of them can lose fortunes while their shrewder fellows get rich.

A further tendency with creative people is to be spontaneous rather than planning. This typically leads them to work in binges or under pressure of deadlines, postpone unpleasant jobs, start too many projects and fail to finish them, or just experience difficulty in making decisions. Because they always want to be 'better informed' before they commit to decisions, this can deepen artistic decisions and give a higher quality to work. The downside to a spontaneous and hedonistic view of life may be lack of organisation, planning, and self control. Beethoven and Van Gogh were two supreme geniuses who lived in chaotic personal environments while their mental processes were of a quality rarely experienced before or since. Again, politicians are the opposite, being largely oriented towards planning, and often – like Stalin – seeing and manipulating circumstances towards their goals several years in advance.

Extraverts are clearly more at home than introverts with the usual social and media requirements of fame. In the heyday of Hollywood this meant satisfying the needs of the Studio's team of publicists. The star was kept constantly in the limelight through premieres, chat shows, appearances at smart night-spots and opening events. Extraverts like to talk more, are often good at greeting people and will typically have a much wider circle of acquaintances. They like being the centre of attention, enjoy variety and action, can act quickly where required, and like having people around them in their working environment. Given that many of the things extroverts thrive on are typical of fame, it is not surprising that the exposure of fame is undoubtedly worse for introverts. Many introverts are supremely talented and work alone contentedly. However, they value privacy, tend to prefer a small number of deep friendships, like to reflect before acting, and dislike interruptions by telephone or otherwise. Meg Tilly has gone on record as saying she quit the acting business because she couldn't stand the assaults on her privacy.

The antidote to uncomfortable media exposure may be a studiously maintained privacy – this worked for Stanley Kubrick and for Greta Garbo. On the advice of Lon Chaney, another recluse, Garbo only went to her first premiere and never answered a fan letter or gave interviews. Although she was thought to be eccentric by Hollywood standards, she had – like many Scandinavians – a dislike of crowds and a preference for a natural and simpler lifestyle, and enjoyed her private life away from the movie world. Louise Rainer expressed the same: "I am a simple person and love the quiet life. But I soon found out I was considered public property. I wasn't emotionally equipped for it. It was like having a picture frame put around me so that everyone could stare at me." (Motion Picture, July 1943) Hollywood was an environment that destroyed the privacy of its inhabitants. As Gene Fowler put it: "Next to privacy, the rarest thing in Hollywood is a wedding anniversary." (Silver Screen, Jan 1943, in McClelland, 1985). This took a particular toll on stars who wanted to be left alone whilst filming: "Seclusion is helpful to most players in the midst of a difficult picture, but it is one of the hardest things to find in busy Hollywood." (Judy Garland, Cue, March 6, 1954, in McClelland, 1985). For that reason, Garbo used to return to Europe in order to recuperate between films.

While introverts particularly dislike intrusions into their privacy, all personality types may resent the desire of the media to 'create' stories about the famous. There is the fear of deliberately hidden aspects of their private life, such as sexual or financial indiscretions, being found out. At any given time, the Press have a number of gossip stories ready for publication once sufficient evidence has been uncovered. There is also the fear that the Press will actually 'create' a story out of nothing, print untruths, or distort events to favour a certain spin. This does happen, and the desire of the famous to litigate may be made easier by recent changes to bring in 'no win no fee' deals. All this causes a significant loss of trust in people who become famous, which adds to the heightened mistrust already seen in performers such as rock musicians (see 16PF scores in Evans, 1994). Press intrusion, fears of being financially exploited and the discomfort of being seen by others as a 'famous' person who can be useful to know, combine to create a powerful cocktail of mistrust – as Heather Ripley (Jemima in 'Chitty Chitty Bang Bang') relates:

"I'm sure if you ask them, 90% of famous people would probably tell you they spend a huge amount of time wishing they could lead private, anonymous lives without the media coverage their every move gets. Being famous is not something you can change when you're tired of it. You can't change your face and start walking around without people recognising you if you suddenly get fed up of the hassle. It's a very isolating experience, you become aware that people will want to know you not because of your own personality and who you are but simply because of your fame, just so they can go round saying 'I know so and so!' That causes distrust of others and can lead to huge problems in relationships. Other problems it causes relationships, is the embarrassment of your private life being splattered all over the papers and feeling you have to hide away in some remote place to get any privacy, not to mention lies being published about you or your partner which kindles the insecurity and distrust of others you're already likely to be suffering from."

A good account of the personality factors referred to above can be found in 'Gifts Differing', which analyses personality types on the Jungian model (Myers and Myers, 1980). There is further data on the performing and creative personality of musicians in Evans, 1994.

THE SELF AND THE IMAGE

"Fame is a form of incomprehension, perhaps the worst." Borges, Pierre Menard, Author of the Quixote (in 'Labyrinths').

Keeping a clear boundary between fantasy and reality is vitally important in handling one's self-image and one's image in the eyes of fans. Performers may go 'into role' for a stage act, adopting particular clothes, another image, even another name. Off-stage they can be confronted by fans or simply ordinary people who still see them 'in role' rather than as themselves. Sometimes the 'roles' are some way away from the real selves.

Shelley Winters was one who felt mis-represented: "I never felt like a blonde bombshell. I have a kind of earthy sexuality, but I'm no great beauty. All the time I was in Hollywood I felt like a fake. That explains the temperament I was known for. Temperament is just another word for terror, and I was terrified at the time because I was being made into something I'm not."

The Press can create a particular image that suits their needs – there always seems to be a place for 'bad boys' like footballer Paul Gascoigne ('Gazza' to the press) or Liam Gallagher of Oasis. The person involved may be less extreme than the image, or can simply change (as when Gazza cut down on his night-club binges in the interests of fitness), so the image becomes outdated. Simply 'being famous' can interfere with 'being normal'. Actress Molly Ringwald explained why she took time off from her movie roles as the archetypal teenage girl to live in Paris for five years by saying: "How long could I have gone on playing Everygirl, when I got so out of the habit of being treated like a normal person?" (Braudy, 1997)

Fame

To some fans you can be yourself, to others you will never be anything other than a public image. Evans recounts a particular instance of this: "I remember sitting at a table with Chet Baker a few months before his death, just after he had played the first set at a jazz club. A journalist came over and asked for an interview, and Chet Baker asked him what he wanted to know. 'Oh, the usual things, why you sound like Miles Davis, why you have a reputation for hard living...' As he got up to sit with the journalist at a quieter table, I said 'It's a shame they never ask you anything personal like 'what's your favourite colour'. 'Yeah,' he said laconically. After the interview he went onto the bandstand and played the whole of the second set. An hour-and-a-half later he came back to the table, sat down, and said 'violet'." (Evans 1994)

One way of maintaining a balanced, familiar self with friends is to take up a hobby. In an environment of mutual interest the star can mix naturally with like-minded people who have other goals and agendas than showbusiness. Golf is an example used by Terry Wogan and many others, though course partners are likely to be sportsmen in ProAm setups or people with money at the very least. Cars are a passion of many rock stars including Elton John and Chris Rea, and toy trains are a consuming interest of Rod Stewart. In fact, rock stars are notorious for their 'boys' toys' – something which probably comes out of playing around with guitars and amplifiers from an early age and yearning for a more stylish conveyance than the band's first beat up Ford Transit.

PAYING ONE'S DUES

"I was appalled to find that when one had come to Hollywood from the theatre, one is supposed to know all about 'acting'. In the theatre it is supposed to take you years and years to learn the rudiments. You don't expect, in your most optimistic moments, to be recognised as a 'star' until you have served a long, gruelling earnest apprenticeship. Here I found that you were a 'star' because someone said you were. It was terrifying." Dorothy McGuire (Photoplay, June 1945, in McClelland, 1985). This terror illustrates the internal worry of not being 'worthy' of fame. The antidote to this is what people in the business call 'paying one's dues' – the work and study needed to 'join the club'.

Sidney Lumet supported the idea that one should have experienced life before trying to act: "In Hollywood actors learn to act from watching television. In New York, people learn to act by walking down the street." Another director put it this way: "I've never yet met a really great actor who was not also a really interesting person." Robert Mitchum said the same: "There are too many pastel people – pastel characters – in Hollywood. They don't know how to portray a character because they don't know people. Some of them are just busy little people studying their lines. If they learned more about life, about people, about psychology, about acting and timing, their characterisations would be more believable. Pastel people can ruin a picture." (Photoplay, Sep 1947, in McClelland, 1985).

Paying one's dues in life, and in the business, forms a solid pedestal for fame. The very word 'work', which people with less than charismatic professions may be shy of, is a magic single syllable in the world of showbiz, and true stars respect it and use it to deepen their command of the medium. "In Hollywood those stars who have been around a long while and seem to grow better with time are the ones who regard 'stardom' merely as an opportunity to grow." (Joseph Cotton, Photoplay, July 1945). The healthy word here is 'grow'.

Work, not glamour, was the cornerstone of Hollywood, and in its heyday it was regular daily work. Although there were many night birds – like Sinatra – who could not adapt to the early 5am starts and the 'daylight hours' of shooting, many others appreciated the evenings at home even though this usually meant learning lines and getting ready for the next day. Some, like Linda Darnell, found that far from the life being one of ease and luxury, she had never worked so hard or so steadily in her entire life. Astute actresses, like Lucille Ball, took this one stage further and realised that she would succeed by 'outworking' everyone else: " I came to Hollywood with twelve showgirls. They had more experience, more money, knew their way around. Yet I made it and they didn't. Why? Maybe because they turned down more working jobs for social opportunities and I did just the opposite. As a result I've never been out of work in this town except for two hours between contracts.* (Ball, 1973)

Carroll Baker recalled the perils involved in turning down work: "I turned down parts and they blacklisted me. It works in an odd way in Hollywood. Joe Schmoe would have lunch with his cronies and say, 'That bitch – she's nothing but trouble – don't hire her!' and pretty soon I couldn't get work" ('People are Crazy Here', 1974, in McClelland,

1985). Even the British were surprised at the pace of work: "In Hollywood everyone seemed to work harder than we did in the English studios, and heaven knows, we worked hard enough." (Anna Neagle, 'There's Always Tomorrow', 1974, in McClelland, 1985).

The moral of these stories is clear – work is healthy, helps one to grow, keeps one in the industry and maintains the fame one has started with.

PROFESSIONAL PRIORITIES

In a healthy order of priorities, the needs of the profession come before the self, and the self comes before other people and audiences. The priorities for a performer are remarkably similar to those taught in many professions, particularly health care:

The Profession: loyalty and respect for your art and profession comes first. This represents its standards, ethics, history and personalities, and the simple joy of performing itself. The great performers, performances or works in any art or sport are always ideals to live up to and a reference when in doubt.

The Self: loyalty to one's own goals and artistic direction is essential, but derives in great part from the best practises of the profession. Using the highest professional standards as a reference keeps personal standards high and the heart in the right place. Personal priorities include mental, physical and artistic self-preservation, and fulfilment of a successful career plan.

Other people: peers in the profession, fellow performers, audiences, teachers, coaches, agents, managers, critics and the press come last. Although they play their part, they come and go in the lives of the famous and should not dominate. As Timothy Gallwey, author of several 'Inner Game' books about mental attitude, says: "the person should play the game, not the game the person."

The reason for this hierarchy is that the profession and the self represent the most constant set of values, while the most variable and unreliable standards are those represented by other people. Respect for the profession and the self enables people to set boundaries such as not performing without thorough technical preparation, not overusing or misusing the body, and not allowing themselves to be needlessly intimidated by fellow performers, audiences, critics or the general public. The only exception to this rule is getting on well with others in the profession. As the American gambler, sportsman and wit Wilson Mizner (1876–1933) first said, and has subsequently been quoted by many famous people, "be nice to people on the way up, because you'll meet them on your way down." (Johnson, 1953)

YOU NEED A STRONG EGO, NOT A BIG EGO

Stars can easily suffer from 'altitude sickness', with its lurking worries 'Am I a fraud? Can I still deliver the goods day in day out? Am I boxing above my weight?' They can easily feel they are higher up in the fame firmament than they are comfortable with, so it is particularly important to have an accurate and believable level of self-esteem. This is equally important in sportspeople, where positive self-esteem helps achieve consistency in the face of competition. As sport psychologist Brian Miller states "Research into the psychology of sport has shown that performance is based around something called the 'success cycle'. The cycle shows the relationship between how you feel about yourself and how you are likely to perform in competition. If you have a positive self image, you are more likely to have a positive attitude which in turn is likely to lead to higher expectations. This usually leads to improved behaviour (going to bed a little earlier or spending more time on preparation) and with these improvements the level of performance increases. Consequently your self-esteem is enhanced and matters progress well." (Bull, 1991)

Self-esteem, however, if we look at all its aspects, is not just something that is 'low' or 'high'. It consists of the 'realistic' part, which is what we are normally capable of doing in practice, but also contains two constant fantasies that influence our hopes, daydreams and worries. We have our 'superior' fantasy of being wonderful, admired, world famous. And we have our 'inferior' fantasy of being useless, a fraud, unable to do simple things well. These fantasies co-exist within us, and we flip from one to the other. "Let's face it – we're all egomaniacs with inferiority complexes" (a quote from an AA meeting) is a succinct way of putting it.

For most, reality sits somewhere in the middle, with our fantasies of being famous above our daily reality level, and our fantasies of being useless below it. For the famous, however, this equation is different. Reality is being famously good at something. There is very little 'superior fantasy' because this has been absorbed by daily reality. The 'inferior' fantasy, however, can be vivid. Whilst fame itself is a confirmation of worth, inner doubt may still question whether such success was either deserved or sustainable. Stars can and have been consumed by this inner doubt. It can hit one early on, later, or at the end of a career. For this reason, famous people need strong egos. What they do not need is 'inflated' egos (too much 'superior' fantasy) which can set the self up for disappointment.

"Hollywood doesn't do anything drastic to people who have strong personalities and firm minds of their own" said Marlene Dietrich. (Modern Screen, the 30s, in McClelland, 1985). The same could be said for musicians like Miles Davis and Duke Ellington, who were legendary for having minds of their own. Strength of ego also refers to the determination to make one's career last once it has begun: "We can't afford to be timid. We can't stand back and be pushed off the rungs of the ladder we have already climbed. Once you let Hollywood push you around, you might as well give up – your prestige as an artist is gone. This business is not famous for its second chances. Once you arrive at the top you've got to fight every moment to stay there. Which is why I never have and never will allow Hollywood to kick me around." Merle Oberon (Photoplay, the 30s, in McClelland, 1985). Betty Hutton was the most succinct: "In Hollywood you've got to scream or they'll shove you around." (Look, Jan 3rd 1950, in McClelland, 1985).

The sense of superiority of the famous can cause both internal and external problems. Envy within the circle of family, friends and social circle – as well as the public at large – is common, and so is the media's reflection of this envy in their attempts to belittle or humiliate those who fall foul of the limelight. People who perceive themselves as superior can also, in the end, pay a high personal price for their ivory tower existence. While practising their careers they have high status in their own eyes and in the eyes of others. As long as they are needed they can play the familiar 'superior' role of exercising their talents and receiving widespread respect in return. But when their careers slide, deprived of their position of power and influence, they can be left as shadows of their former prestigious selves.

Isolated by the familiarity of feeling superior to others and unable to let go of that fundamental ego position, such stars no longer have any way of actually proving this superiority on a day-to-day social basis. Maintaining the company of such fellow professionals as are still within their social circle, they may be unable to create new or meaningful relations with others who they continue to perceive as below their station in life, and may in a number of cases resort to drink and relative seclusion. The term 'limelight deprivation' has been used to describe this withdrawal from the nourishment of fame. As death – the great leveller – approaches, they find in their intellectual seclusion that the grim reaper gives them no preferential treatment, and they are as alone and powerless as the next person, however lowly their station. Actors, who know more than most the fleeting and unpredictable nature of work, will always say that they have been 'lucky'. It keeps their options open, and absolves them from self blame if or when the work dries up.

WHAT IS THE MOTIVATION OF THE FAMOUS?
Work appears easy to those who really enjoy it, so how does a psychologist actually analyse how motivated people are by their work? One useful system employed in sport psychology is primary and secondary motivation (Bull, 1991). Primary motivation is enjoying something for its own sake – the air passing by as one runs, the excitement of downhill skiing, the sheer beautiful sound of music. Secondary motivation describes the incidental benefits, such as winning, having one's name in the papers, being on television or meeting famous people. As Gregory Peck stated, primary motivation is the best insurance in the fame business: "I think because of my stage training and my years in New York I had a respect for the craft of acting and a fascination with it, so that the intent to do work of top quality was always of more interest to me than being a movie star. I can honestly say I never went off the rails on becoming a celebrity." (Boller and Davis, 1987)

Talent is a firm base for fame even in the case of the docusoaps. Stars of the British docusoaps 'Cruise' and 'Clampers' had previous performing careers and were quite ready for the overnight fame they received. But for some people there is no doubt that the primary motivation is fame itself. Desire for attention may be behind Page Three modelling work, for example, but this may be a flash in the pan if there is no talent to back it up – what does one do next? Where there is performing talent, as with Melinda Messenger or Samantha Fox, then the career can become solid. Where there remains confusion as to what to be famous for, there is a real risk of exploitation. The exhibitionism behind some forms of modelling, for example, is quite in harmony with the needs of the porn industry.

As Dr Richard Cox says, "Theoretically it should be easy to distinguish between primary and secondary sources of motivation for one need ask but one question, which is 'when all the obvious sources of secondary motivation are removed, does the person concerned continue with the activity?'" (Bull, 1991) Musicians who simply love making music do frequently continue long after their overnight hits pale into obscurity. Famous people who transfer their allegiance to secondary benefits like making money, however, may prefer to go down that path through making investments and opening businesses. Primary motivation may then shift to making money or enjoying life in the business world, or in some cases becoming successful in politics.

WOMEN INTO MANAGEMENT – THE CHANGING ROLE OF THE FEMALE STARS

"Women stars in Hollywood were invariably in one of two categories – women who were exploited by men and the much smaller group of women who survived by acting like men" said Otto Preminger. ('Preminger', 1977) Those who remember Rex Harrison in 'My Fair Lady' saying "Why can't a woman be more like a man" will remember his reasons – men are so much more 'reasonable'. This agrees with the Myers Briggs database (Myers and Myers, 1980) which shows that two thirds of men are 'reasoning' while two thirds of women are 'feeling'. But while charisma may contain a raft of emotionally based character traits, business skills require cold and effective analysis – no doubt of the kind that Preminger was referring to as a male characteristic.

It is no longer a case of 'dizzy or diligent' – the effervescent Goldie Hawn is only one whose deceptive girlie front conceals a first class business brain. Women want both sides of the equation – the feminine and the businesslike, be that masculine in the stereotypical sense or simply effective in the true sense of the word. It is more a case of values than sex – women often have the same values of power, control and equality at the highest level, and are not afraid to demand them. Moreover, there have been no shortage of intelligent female stars – Elizabeth Shue and Mira Sorvino are Harvard alumni, Angela Bassett, Jennifer Connelly, Jodie Foster, Meryl Streep and Jennifer Beals are Yale. Oxford and Cambridge alumni run into double figures. Geena

Davis, Sharon Stone, Veleka Gray and Asia Carrera are Mensa members, while Jill St John is reputed to have an IQ of 165. The famous women who have taken out patents – some very lucrative – include Hedy Lamarr for radio controlled devices like torpedoes, and Julie 'The Catwoman' Newmar for pantyhose.

Leading women stars who have demonstrated particularly astute business acumen include Mae West who owned a big chunk of Los Angeles when she died and Diana Ross who part owns Motown. Norwegian skater and actress Sonja Henie died one of the ten wealthiest women in the world. Oprah Winfrey controls enormous assets including those of her shows, and stands to make $130,000,000 for continuing her talk show through the 1999–2000 TV season.

QUESTIONING THE GLASS CEILING

The term glass ceiling has typically been used to describe the invisible attitude barrier women perceive as blocking their path into management and other traditionally male areas of business. However, its usefulness goes way beyond this. It is, in fact, a particularly good term for describing the ceiling all of us put on our perceived chances in life, our abilities, our social status and how accepted we are by others. Often people are prevented from enjoying the luxuries of life by their own attitudes and self-imposed psychological restrictions (we understand good value for money), the benefits of a higher social world (we know our place in life), the benefits of high earning (we've never been good at money) or the enjoyment of skills they could master (we're bad at maths, are tone deaf, cannot act, write and so on).

One would assume that those comfortable with fame have a very high glass ceiling, and want to continue life at the top level, but this may not be true in all respects. Famous people still eat in the kitchen, like Sir Paul McCartney, hand over their accounts completely to people they hope they can trust, and shop in supermarkets. Many have to persuade themselves that they can be good at something apart from their primary skill – actors who learn to write plays (Harold Pinter) or sing (Marilyn Monroe), singers who become songwriters (Stevie Wonder) or actors (Frank Sinatra), musicians who learn to produce (Quincy Jones), conduct (Ashkenazy, Rostropovich) or compose (Rachmaninov).

Fame

Inside many famous people lie other parallel skills, and increasingly they are starting to diversify and use these skills. They may use the leverage they have through their fame to create further opportunities which use their inherent qualities like creativity, intelligence, imagination and charisma. Actors have benefited from the breakdown of the big Studio system through being able to direct and produce their own projects. Technology, whilst more advanced, is smaller and cheaper, work can be done at home with computers, de-centralising of skills is ongoing, and the self-help movement has accentuated self-actualisation. The healthy benefits of diversifying include freshness and variety, avoidance of burnout, and a new lease of creative life.

REFERENCES

Ball, Lucille (1973) *Lucy*

Braudy, Leo (1997) *The Frenzy of Renown – Fame and its History*, NY, Vintage Books

Boller, Paul F Jr and Davis, Ronald L (1987) *Hollywood Anecdotes*, London, Macmillan

Bull, Stephen J (1991) *Sport Psychology*, Marlborough Wilts. UK, The Crowood Press

Evans, Andrew (1994) *The Secrets of Musical Confidence*, London, HarperCollins

Holmes, TH and Rahe, RH (1967) *The social readjustment rating scale*, Journal of Psychosomatic Research, 11:213–18

Johnson, A (1953) *The Incredible Mizners*

McClelland, Doug (1985) *Hollywood on Hollywood – Tinsel Town Talks* Winchester MA USA:

Myers, IB and PB(1980) *Gifts Differing*, Palo Alto, Consulting Psychologists Press

Preminger, O (1977) *An Autobiography*

FAME IN THE FAMILY

T he Sly Stone hit tells us "It's a family affair". Everyone has a family background, and the famous are no exception. But famous people attract a lot of attention, exist in a world where ambition and envy are constant companions, and create models of success that may be difficult to live up to. As a result, there are endless examples of families and relationships that have been emotionally restructured around the needs of talented individuals. There have been classic cases of neglect or over-dominance by parents, but several other cases where gifted individuals have transcended all manner of difficulties. We know this to be true through the obvious fact that they made it to the top.

CHILD STARS

"Public adoration is the greatest thing in the world." Jackie Coogan NY Herald Tribune, Jan 30th 1958 (Cary, 1978)

Hollywood child actors have a special place in the annals of famous children. The concept of 'the child' as portrayed on screen is, in fact, relatively recent. Throughout history, children were treated as little adults – in a tougher kind of world they had to help where they could, and often worked hard. Charles Dickens was one of the writers who exposed both the hardships of children and the pathos of childhood, often through unforgettable figures like Oliver Twist and David Copperfield, and worse still through those cases (as with Tiny Tim in 'A Christmas Carol' and Smike in 'Nicholas Nickleby') where death could be a merciful release from tragic lives of suffering. In such a period of child mortality from then prevalent diseases like scarlet fever and diphtheria, children were easily perceived as 'little angels'. With some foresight, Dickens even portrayed a ruthlessly driven child stage act, 'The Infant Phenomenon' in 'Nicholas Nickleby', who in true Hollywood tradition was perennially ten years old. Little Ninetta Crummles was actually 15, but remained small in stature as a result of late nights and "an unlimited diet of gin and water".

Although being routinely put to work is exactly what happened to the first child stars, they created an aura of being special. By the 1860s – the decade Lewis Carroll was immortalising childhood in Britain – Lotta Crabtree, the first child stage act with her appealing curls and bravely dramatic song and dance routine, was forging a special magnetism with the rough male communities of 49ers in the California Gold Rush. Much later, child actor Elsie Janis was to develop a special bond with the soldiers of WW1 in much the same way. By 1921 the child actor craze had established itself in Hollywood, spearheaded by the success of Jackie Coogan, who was earning $22,500 a week at his peak and in 1923 topped even Valentino and Fairbanks in the popularity polls. During the Golden Years of 1925 to 1945, the rush to get one's child into the movies was such that the 'Our Gang' series interviewed 140,000 children in seventeen years. Of these, only 176 appeared on screen and only 41 were put under contract at salaries no higher than $75 per week. Even then, the crowded auditions managed to reject Mickey Rooney and Shirley Temple.

The years following the Second World War changed the image of the child yet again. The cheesy idea of children gave way to a new child actor who was more vulnerable, and whose characters had more depth – Elizabeth Taylor, Hayley Mills, Tatum O'Neal, Patty Duke. The baby boom that followed the war meant that parents had also had enough of their own children in real life to want to see them so often in movies. Therefore, the child actor boom thinned out from 1945 onwards, as some of the reality of life began to affect even Hollywood, and European films like 'The Bicycle Thieves' crossed the pond.

Hollywood may never have surpassed the pathos of some of the best post-war portrayals of children in European cinema: the child stars of films by Fellini and Truffaut, Hayley Mills and the children in many classic British adaptations of the original Dickens stories that did so much to start the interest in children in the first place. Celebrated Hollywood children of more recent times have included Brooke Shields (with a 'movie mother' the equal of any before) and McCauley Culkin, whose family litigation over control of his assets proved that little had changed there since the twenties.

THE 'MOVIE PARENTS'

From the earliest times in the history of child actors, fathers had a habit of either dying in the formative years of the child (Charlie Chaplin's father when he was a boy and Judy Garland's when she was 13), constantly disappearing (Lotta Crabtree's father) or being dismissed by the stage and movie mothers (Ginger Rogers' father McGrath). They were largely redundant to the symbiosis of mother and child, whatever psychological side effects this deprivation may have caused. Even when they were present, they were often unemployed because of the depression, as in the case of Shirley Temple's father, or simply dominated by their formidable wives. They could sometimes be as much of a problem for the child as a support – as Jackie Coogan's father joked, "In business, don't even trust your own father". Like the movie mothers, they tended to exploit their offspring financially or, as a result of their famous child, by trying to get into the movies themselves. Jackie Coogan claimed that his father "wound up playing six parts in 'The Kid', moved up to being Charlie Chaplin's assistant and was earning $150 a week to his son's $75". (Cary 1978)

The 'Movie Mothers' were a race unto themselves – well deserving of the 'Hollywood Movie Mother of the Year' awards created uniquely for their benefit. Fiercely possessive of their offspring, they had formidable manipulative and managerial skills – none more so than Gertrude Temple, who became a well-paid studio fixture as her daughter's 'coach' and 'hairdresser'. Lela Rogers controlled all aspects of Ginger's career, and Charlotte Pickford was jokingly referred to as running the United Artists set whilst Mary was filming. They were totally single minded in making their offspring work hard – Gertrude Temple's recipe for success was "There is no argument, no pleading and begging. I have never permitted any impudence, crying or display of temper. I soon learned not to let my affection make me too lenient." ('Mrs Temple on bringing up Shirley', Parent's Magazine, October 1938 – in Cary 1978). The reasoning behind such total control was often that if anyone was going to control their daughter, ensuring her best interests were protected and that she came to no harm at the hands of others, the controller should be the mother. While the danger of exploitation by others was real, the option of teaching the child to control things herself does not seem to have entered the equation.

In the early days the mothers got their business sense from wheeling and dealing – Mary Ann Crabtree in the camps of the California Gold Rush (losing $27,000 in one business gamble), and Charlotte Smith (Pickford), mother of 'Baby Gladys' – later Mary Pickford – in the fish markets of Toronto. They got their driving ambition from two main motivations. First, getting out of poverty and into riches. Most of the movie mothers started in relative poverty, so status and money became for them an addictive drug – even if it was to be achieved through their offspring's talents. These mothers later used their wealth to buy status symbols – chief of which was a mansion to live out their stage-struck lives in, with grandiose titles like Crabtree's 'Attol Tryst' and Janis' 'Manor House' – every bit as impressive as the 'Pickfair' created by the child star Mary Pickford and Douglas Fairbanks.

The other driving ambition of the 'Movie Mothers' was to live out their own desires for drama, adulation and fame through their offspring. Some, like the parents of Chaplin and Jackie Coogan, were already stage professionals. Others used their children to further their own roles in showbusiness. They could be grandiosely melodramatic by nature, like Jenny Janis in her "pompadoured chestnut hair" and plumed velvet hats. Others were simply thwarted in their own desire for fame, like Rose Hovick – mother of Gypsy Rose Lee and June Havoc – who once shouted at June to "get out of my dressing room", adding ironically "I've spent my whole life on you." (Cary, 1978) The famous survived this emotional hot house, but many were children who were needlessly pushed by parents seeking fame by proxy into performing careers for which they were unsuited – as portrayed in Noel Coward's song 'Don't put your daughter on the stage, Mrs Worthington'.

'Mother knew best' in the majority of cases. Sometimes, quite simply, 'Mother was all'. Shirley Temple's 1988 autobiography ended with the simple words "Thanks Mom". Lotta Crabtree's public farewell to her mother contained the words "What I am, what I have been, what I was, I owe entirely to my mother, the most wonderful woman that ever lived – and I want the world to know it". But this perception of the 'giving mother' was far from the whole truth. The role confusion was considerably more profound. Often the mother who had 'given her life for the daughter' was no more descriptive of reality than the daughter who had 'given her whole life up to the ambition of the mother'. This resulted in a peculiar symbiotic inter-dependence that spawned a multitude of psychologically strange phenomena, maybe none stranger than Baby Peggy's mother actually taking on her daughter's stage name of Peggy Montgomery to do extra work with Central Casting after her daughter had left the movies.

The mother's possessiveness would brook no interference, either with the financial or artistic affairs of the daughter. Everyone was a potential rival for power – from agents to studio bosses, to other child stars. With their own identities completely dwarfed by the fame of their offspring, these earth-shifting people-consuming 'martyred' mothers were in truth guarding a self-created goldmine by tooth and by claw. And woe betide any good looking young man who threatened the family silver: "If Mary Ann Crabtree had drawn a ring of fire around her Lotta, Jenny Janis had surrounded Elsie – a thirty eight year old spinster – with a moat that no man had yet had the temerity to cross." As Elsie herself said: "Several well-meaning friends tried to break the combination (of mother and daughter) but some optimist tried to chisel his way into the Bank of England once." (Cary, 1978) When the moat was actually crossed, the reaction of Ginger Rogers' stunned mother, sitting with her handkerchief screwed up in her hand, was "I still can't believe she would do this to me."

What the 'ungrateful' daughter was doing, ironically, was not only living out her natural sexual urges but, more particularly, following all the romantic ideals that had been put into her head by the movie industry itself. Elizabeth Taylor was not the only one who "sought movielike solutions to problems. If a story did not end happily, Elizabeth would interrupt and say 'Oh, don't end it this way, I want it to end happily'" (Cary, 1978) As Baby Peggy said, "If other children of our generation grew up watching movies and were deeply influenced by their false values, those of us whose childhoods were marinaded in Hollywood sentimentality were even more addicted to the lie."(Cary, 1978) Ironically, in another way child stars were deprived of the make-believe of normal children. "I stopped believing in Santa Claus at an early age", recalls Shirley Temple. "Mother took me to see him in a Hollywood department store, and he asked me for my autograph." (Shirley Temple, 1975, in McClelland, 1985).

PSYCHOLOGICAL EFFECTS ON CHILD ACTORS

The psychological mix-ups in this interdependent relationship are legion. For a start, child actors were detached from the natural growth into adulthood of other neighbourhood children and the normal give and take of social relationships. They did not make small talk with people their own age, and had to compete day in and day out for work, suffering the contentious and divisive atmosphere created on and off the set by parents and movie people. Their education was rudimentary, until the advent of the early Fame Schools like Lawlor's Professional School, and even then they grew up in a hot house of other child stars where the school was a glorified studio set. "Lawlor's looked like the prop department's idea of a school. School hours only took up half the day, since interviews were rarely held in the morning hours. There were about ten rooms scattered around a main hall, and most of them were equipped with wall mirrors, practise bars and pianos. By one o'clock the classrooms had been cleared for action. For the rest of the afternoon and evening everyone was practising juggling, tap routines, ballet, opera, blues, piano, violin, diction and contortions. Even the school telephone was an extension of the casting agencies." (Cary, 1978) Welfare agencies were often thwarted in their attempts to help: a five year old who could earn $2000 a week without being able to read or write did not, on the face of it, need an education.

More dangerous were the stunts that children were required to do on set, such as the tragedy that occurred on a late-night location for 'Twilight Zone: The Movie' in 1982: "While working illegally, after hours and without the required child welfare representatives on the set, two small Vietnamese children were killed while their stricken parents looked on when a helicopter pilot lost control. There followed a sensational trial in which the jury brought in a verdict of 'not guilty'. Ironically, in the aftermath, California child labour laws were not tightened but actually relaxed: younger children are now permitted to work later hours than before and permission has even been given to work school-age children after midnight." (Cary, 1978)

Rules for the protection of children on set were drawn up by the Humane Society, but their parents still retained control of them in the legal sense, retaining their entitlement for their custody, income and services. This meant that they were financially exploited as a result. "Nearly every one of us was an innocent where money was concerned, having handed over every cent we earned to our parents since we were infants. And in most cases our parents worked to keep us ignorant of financial matters, not even showing us how to make out a cheque or deposit slip on our own." (Cary, 1978) One amendment was made as a result of Jackie Coogan losing almost his entire fortune to those who had custody of it after his father's death. The 'Coogan Act' required parents to put aside at least half of the child's earnings, but even this did not prevent parents from 'investing' the child's income at the rate of up to $1000 per week.

Child actors frequently ended up effectively penniless at the end of a profitable career. Edith Fellows on her twenty first birthday "returned to Hollywood to collect her childhood earnings, held in trust by a California bank under the terms of the Coogan Act and received a cheque for exactly $900.60 – the amount she had earned every week at Columbia. Tragic though it was, Edith's story had a familiar ring that made it almost commonplace." (Cary 1978) Nor have things improved significantly. Heather Ripley, who was only seven when she played Jemima in 'Chitty Chitty Bang Bang' (1968) said "I wish I could sue for compensation. It was child exploitation. I can't listen to that awful accent they made me use without squirming and they paid me peanuts. Most people assume I get money every time it's shown and must be rich. In fact I only got six or seven thousand after it had been invested for ten years."

Prevented from acquiring an adult sense of money, child actors were required in a general sense to keep their childhood going for years after they had physically outgrown it – claiming, paradoxically, that they had never had a childhood at all. Many felt pushed into a movie career they had never wanted – "there's a difference between walking on stage and being pushed from behind", as one star put it. They developed stage fright as a result of being dropped into situations they could barely manage, despite the commonly held assumption that children never suffer stage fright. Worse still, they experienced several problems through confusing their movie personality with their real identity, to the point where they ended up literally hating their movie persona: "I felt as though a long delayed time bomb had finally detonated and what self-esteem I possessed was disintegrating all around me. I loathed everyone and everything that was even associated with Hollywood. My wrath turned inward, beaming its murderous rage toward someone I had come to hate more than anyone else in he world – Baby Peggy. She was the one who had done it all to me. She was the one who kept me captive, without any self of my own. She was the one I would have to destroy if I was to survive." (Cary 1978)

Those that enjoyed childhood fame were vulnerable to problems like suicide, underage sex and addiction to drugs and alcohol. Given such a strange role reversal with their parents whereby they 'parented' their own parents, both financially and emotionally, it is hardly surprising that the lives of child actors are a unique psychological case study in themselves. Many sought whatever therapeutic help was close at hand in order to resolve their identity crises. This could range from three years of counselling from Dr Arnold Hutschnecker (author of 'The Will to Live') in the case of Jackie Cooper, to analysis in the case of Dickie Moore. Christian Science was a refuge for Marcia Mae Jones and the Catholic Church for Baby Peggy, who stated that "Although no longer living under my parents roof I found I still could not free myself from the lifelong pattern of wanting to make them happy by giving them money. Perhaps I still needed to feel essential to their happiness in order to feel loved." (Cary, 1978)

Many found it difficult to form emotional attachments later on in life. Diana Serra Cary's first husband had "married Baby Peggy", not herself. "Marriage had represented a psychologically imperative 'come-back'. It must prove to everyone – most of all ourselves – that, washed up though we might seem at eighteen or twenty, we were intelligent adults who could make a success of the most important career in life – matrimony. I believe the terrible sense of failure that we child stars carried over from adolescence made the failure of our marriages a far more devastating experience than outsiders might imagine it to be. Divorce only re-projected on a still wider screen the original break-down of our childhood image. I for one had no idea of who I was or where I was going. All I knew was who I had once been and that was a tough act to follow." (Cary, 1978). Other child actors married several times – seven in the case of Mickey Rooney, eight in the case of Elizabeth Taylor. Some only found happiness well away from their pasts, Deanna Durbin settled in France with her third husband, and Heather Ripley fled to Ireland and hid away for years to avoid attention after 'Chitty Chitty Bang Bang'.

Ultimately, child stars were set free and re-introduced to genuine childhood by their own children. Many vowed never to put them through the same: "Not surprisingly, nearly every former child star I know has displayed a fierce desire to protect his or her own children from the limelight. Perhaps we do it not merely for the sake of our children but because we know instinctively that we need their carefree and happy childhoods every bit as much as they do – probably a great deal more." (Cary, 1978). Baby Peggy's eye-opening and largely autobiographical account of child actors, recounted under her adult name Diana Serra Cary in 'Hollywood's Children', applies mainly to the

147-10

ELVIS PRESLE

Elvis Presley - Elvis was one of several superstars for whom premature death led to canonisation and resurrection fantasies.

Brigitte Bardot - actresses whose success is based on youthful good looks and sex appeal have particular problems in coping with ageing.

Greta Garbo - one response to media intrusion is to become reclusive. This can have the paradoxical effect of increasing public interest.

James Dean - stars often crystallise psychological needs and personality types - in Dean's case, teenage rebelliousness.

Marlon Brando - charisma is a magical presence that derives from a combination of looks, voice and body language.

Madonna - single-minded determination and skilled image management can elevate moderately talented individuals to the status of superstars.

Leonardo DiCaprio - some stars appeal to particular target audiences. In the case of the baby-faced DiCaprio it is primarily teenage girls.

Sigourney Weaver - today's heroines are expected to bear weapons and fight aliens with the best of men.

Clark Gable - many of the great Hollywood stars effectively played themselves, in Gable's case a handsome "tomcat" who took women on his own terms yet made them feel feminine at the same time.

heyday of Hollywood. Later child stars may have been spared some of the hot-house atmosphere and excesses of that period, but much of what they recount covers the same ground. Here is a similar quote from child actor Michael F Blake:

"Speaking as a former child actor I can confirm that we don't retire. We are forced out of a job by growing up. We are then put into the unenviable position of having to choose a new direction for our life and career. We got very little career advice – some child actors might have gotten advice from older actors or directors on a personal level, but none ever got any advice on a general level from the unions (SAG or AFTRA) in Los Angeles. The industry should do more for child performers, but sadly they never will. Some go on to use drugs, rob dry cleaners, appear on TV chat shows and generally say to the world "feel sorry for me, I'm no longer important". Then there are those who either move into fields behind the cameras (I became a makeup artist) or just simply move on to other fields, raise a family and live a pretty "normal" life. Make no mistake about it, being a child actor can be tough. Your career is pretty limited time-wise. And it can play on your psyche when you are no longer needed by the film and TV industry. Happily, there are more former child actors out there living a normal life than the ones who make the cover of the National Enquirer."

Heather Ripley – who left the movie business completely after appearing in 'Chitty Chitty Bang Bang' – is not so optimistic: "The stress of the whole ordeal traumatised me so much that I have Attention Deficit Disorder, which I didn't have before the film. I can't hold down a job or keep relationships together, I have very poor organisational skills, I suffer from mood swings, anxiety, paranoia, stress, depression and alcoholism and have been through a couple of periods of drug addiction. My parent's divorce was doubly difficult for me as it was partly caused by them being separated for 14 months during the filming, which I internalised a lot of blame for, and subsequently I was effectively alienated from my entire family with the exception of my father and grandmother. I have only recently got to grips with most of my problems after six years counselling at the Findhorn Foundation, and have re-established a good relationship with my mother, who did not speak to me for 10 years. Kids should absolutely not be encouraged by their parents to seek fame at an early age. Fame, in itself, has little benefit and many disadvantages. I think that if I had continued as an actress – though I am a damn good actress – I would be dead or insane." This is a particularly poignant illustration of the dangers of experiencing too much fame too fast, where a child from a small village community whose parents have no knowledge of the film business is catapulted into a major role. This demonstrates the need to stagger significant life changes and learn the ins and outs of the business first, as described in the Chapter 5. It also shows yet again the effects on the larger family unit when the mother bonds closely with the daughter due to the filming, and how an emotionally immature child's mind can internalise blame when things go wrong.

THE MUSICAL CHILD PRODIGY
There are innumerable instances in the classical music world of child prodigies – in fact, a large number of virtuosi started their instruments early and then made rapid progress. Violinist Jascha Heifetz played the Mendelssohn Concerto aged seven in public and debuted officially in St. Petersburg aged eleven. When Heifetz debuted in the US at seventeen the violinist Mischa Elman, sitting with the pianist Godowsky (himself a prodigy by age three), turned to him and said "Don't you find it hot in here – shall we take the air?" to which he replied "Mischa, it's not hot for pianists". Menuhin was another violin prodigy, and appeared with the teenage conductor Lorin Maazel. Fritz Kreisler debuted aged ten and toured for five years as a prodigy. He then stopped playing in public for ten years. Several pianists were child prodigies, like Albeniz, who gave his first recital aged four, Field who debuted in Dublin aged six, Liszt who debuted aged eight and conquered Vienna at eleven, and Solomon, whose talent was exploited young. Arrau describes the psychological effects of early exposure to the spotlight in "Conversations with Arrau" (Joseph Horowitz). He was only one of several who underwent extensive and prolonged psychoanalysis after his childhood years.

On the other hand there were pianists like Josef Hoffman, one of the most exploited of child prodigies, who made a stunning debut aged six, waited until age nine before touring Europe (playing solo pieces and Beethoven's 1st Piano Concerto under Blow), and made his New York debut at 11. His appetite for concerts was such that within three months in the US, he had played 16 concerts at the Met and 24 on tour. When the Society for the Prevention of Cruelty to Children forced him to cancel 40 remaining concerts he was furious – he adored appearing in public and insisted throughout his life that his early concerts had not tired or over-taxed him. His later career was highly distinguished, and he founded the Curtis Music Institute. In his book on playing the piano, he advocated quality of life and adequate leisure time – maintaining one hour's practice per day was enough. This, coupled with the fact that he had wide interests and was an inventor with more than 70 patents to his name, may have helped him avoid burnout. By his late teens, Vladimir Horowitz had a repertoire of over 200 pieces, and at the age of 20 played no less than 25 separate recitals in St Petersburg alone without repeating a single work. His later life, however, was dogged by periods away from performing, and one wonders whether this white heat of performing early on was a cause. The frenzy of performing in concert, in the aftermath of International Competition wins, has certainly drained a number of young artists prematurely.

Composers were even more impressive – Carl Maria von Weber wrote an opera at the age of nine, Felix Mendelssohn had memorised all the Beethoven symphonies and could play them on the piano aged eight. The incredible early talents of Mozart are well known, but much less known are those of his sister Marianne – like Mendelssohn's sister Fanny – who was also an extremely gifted musician, and impressed audiences alongside Wolfgang at their family concerts. As a woman at that time, she was married off by father Leopold to the wealthy Johann Freiherr von Berchtold zu Sonnenburg. Wolfgang congratulated his sister: "man rules by day, and women by night". It seems that little Wolfgang elbowed himself quite energetically into her piano-lessons from an early age. As soon as his father perceived his very unusual talents, he switched the bulk of his didactic skills to his son in order to make him an accomplished musician able to serve at any court in Europe. Marianne was simply a prodigy, Wolfgang was a prodigy with a future. By promoting his infant treasure, his father was no different from the indomitable 'Movie Mothers' of Hollywood. Psychoanalysts have suggested that the dominance of Mozart's career by his ambitious father was motivated by his seeking to achieve, through his son, the musical fame that had eluded him (Sterin, 1990). A perceptive study of Mozart's youth and education can be found in Elias, 1993.

In the popular music world, children sometimes debuted in family groups, as Michael Jackson did in the Jackson 5. The hours were long and the work hard, with constant tours, concerts and recording sessions. It is not impossible for burnout to occur even by one's teens, and Jackson, like Stevie Wonder, is lucky to have taken his talent right through to his adult years. It is all too easy to overlook the fact that a star who is famous at ten has, by the tender age of 30, already been in the business for 20 years. Child musicians shared many of the difficulties of child actors: hard work at an early age, ambitious parents, burnout or periods off performing, and therapy in later life. The big difference is that there is no cut off point when the child grows into an adult, except in rare cases like boy sopranos, where the early careers of Ernest Lush and Aled Jones, for instance, did not continue on the same level after the voice broke.

There has been much debate over the question of what family experiences are most likely to promote the appearance of genius in musical and other creative fields. Some argue that the hothouse treatment can turn an averagely talented individual into a high flier, whilst others argue that the emergence of genius is unpredictable and mysterious – much more of an innate talent unfolding from within. Interestingly, Mozart's case has been cited by proponents of both theories, since it has elements of both. What is clear is that persons who are truly eminent (those who make exceptional creative contributions) tend to come from families that are different from those of mere "high achievers" (Albert, 1996).

Another theory is that creative genius is enhanced by the provision of freedom and the encouragement of spontaneity, while standard achievement may be more a product of parental pushing and hard graft (Sloboda, 1990). The latest research from McGill University, however, refutes both the hothouse and the freedom theories, and finds only one common factor in the backgrounds of creative people – that of parental conflict in the preschool years. It suggests that children brought up by warring parents may give up looking for praise from authority figures and plough their own furrow – a hallmark of creative originality (Richard Koestner, 1999, in Journal of Research in Personality). Human creativity as a whole is such a complex phenomenon, however, that it is likely that no single influence would dominate.

CHILDREN IN SPORT
While most sports are adult at the élite levels, there are some – notably

tennis and gymnastics – where top stars such as Olga Korbut compete while still young. Sport psychologists have, therefore, paid particular attention to the needs of the younger competitor. The coach relationship is particularly important at this age because of the time spent together and the parental role played by the coach. So is the principle, as with child actors, that despite their entertainment value to the media world, children in sport have specific educational and emotional needs that must be protected. In the case of competitive physical sports, there is the added importance of ensuring that children take no harmful drugs that may affect their growth.

One crucial factor that needs to be built into training is the building and preservation of positive self-esteem, through frequent rewards, mixing pleasurable activities with more boring physical ones and ensuring a graded progress where there is the chance to do well and reach and surpass set goals. It is also important to put winning, and competition in general, into a context of enjoying the whole range of activities within the sport, including daily training and team spirit.

Former gymnast and lecturer in sport psychology Misia Gervis describes how competitive stress can be reduced: "One of the key factors in reducing stress is to shift the emphasis away from the outcome of the competition towards the performance. Children need constant recognition of their own abilities and they should not be left to compare themselves to other athletes. By giving the athlete feedback about the positive element of their performance, and eliminating negative thoughts, the athlete will feel more confident. Another important factor involves ensuring that both coach and athlete have realistic expectations. Children often get false ideas of their potential from adults. Sometimes the parents have inflated expectations, and sometimes the coaches. Either way it can be a potential source of stress for the child." (Bull, 1991) Movie mothers all over again?

CHILDREN OF FAMOUS PARENTS

Having a famous parent may be something of a 'sink or swim' situation. Those who stayed afloat are actors like Michael Douglas, Kiefer Sutherland, Jane and Peter Fonda and Liza Minelli. Yet even these kids with famous names had to come up the hard way and prove they could act. Likewise, popular musicians like Julian Lennon and classical musicians like Igor Oistrakh (violin) and Dennis Brain (horn) had to prove they could play the same instrument as their father, the latter easily surpassing his father's already fine reputation.

Since comparisons are inevitable when parents and children do the same thing for a living, the child may have an easier time of it in a different field altogether. Stella McCartney has demonstrated this in the world of fashion design, succeeding Karl Lagerfeld at Paris fashion house Chloe in 1997. While the press avoided actually saying that her father, Sir Paul, had anything to do with her speedy rise in the fashion firmament, they certainly speculated and waited for her to prove herself, which she did conclusively enough by increasing Chloe's sales five fold since her appointment.

At its best, a childhood in the family of the rich and famous can have many benefits. Showbiz can be exciting for kids, with its film sets, parties, charismatic family friends and holidays in interesting company and exclusive places. It also has career perks as Paul Clemens recalled: "Being Eleanor Parker's son never got me any parts, but it did get me an agent at age thirteen – hers. We still share him." (Cary, 1978) Research has shown that performance studies students without parents in the profession are more likely to suffer low self-esteem, require therapy and fail in their training, which supports this point of view (Hamilton, 1997).

On the other hand, having parents in the profession can also bring a raft of problems. If the performer's needs compete with those of talented siblings or successful parents then professional development may be impeded. Parents may often be away, leaving children with a succession of home helps, and feeling cruelly ignored and sidelined (Mitchell and Cronson, 1987). Many showbiz marriages break up, resulting in one set of step-parents, brothers and sisters after another. In an atmosphere already rife with competition and attention, jealousy and envy may become a big problem. It can even pass down from one generation to another. Judy Garland described her own mother as "the real life wicked witch of the West", yet she was at times just as vindictive with her daughter Liza Minelli. As her own health and career deteriorated, she became jealous and hostile towards Liza, who showed signs of replacing her in popularity. Liza lived in the shadow of Judy for much of her performing years and later (like her mother) developed drug problems, (Spada, 1983).

Knafo (1991) explored the dynamics of children who grow up with famous or infamous parents in areas such as show business, literature, science and politics. Her data revealed "a paradoxical picture of privilege and neglect that creates narcissistic wounds, ambivalent and magical identifications and difficulties moving out of the famous parents' shadow to establish a mature sense of identity." Children of infamous parents experienced the added burden of having to defend and justify their parents' misdeeds.

Although psychoanalysts are inclined to search for psychopathology rather than adaptiveness, it does seem that growing up with celebrity parents has its disadvantages as well as advantages.

Children of the wealthy and famous seem to be at greater risk of drug abuse than those from ordinary families (Wellisch, 1984). Possible causes for this include parental absence or failure to pay attention, and failure to provide an intact system of self-esteem. As with child actors, the best parents for ensuring the success of their children are likely to be the pushy doting ones who move mountains for their offspring, not parents who have very busy professional lives of their own.

SIBLINGS AND FAME

There is a certain solidarity in becoming famous with your brothers and sisters, as several musical acts have shown, including the Bee Gees, The Osmonds, The Carpenters and more recently Hansen, Bewitched and The Corrs. Most sibling bands are very close – not only genetically but also emotionally and stylistically – though strong willed brothers can fall out at times, as the Gallaghers have done in Oasis. Some groups like the Brubecks included the father, and the generation gap in these cases may or may not achieve the same closeness of purpose. Very different are the families where one or more sibling is famous, and the others are not, or are much less well known. Some died mysteriously, like Lotta Crabtree's brother Ashworth who was "lost at sea" following heavy drinking, and Elsie Janis' brother Percy who even managed to shoot himself before falling overboard. Mary Pickford's brother Jack, after heavy drinking, was pronounced dead in hospital just outside Paris aged 36. Surviving with a famous sibling seems to have been more than some could manage.

Fame

Then there were the siblings who tried and failed, like Baby Peggy's sister Louise, a sensitive child two and a half years older than her and initially their father's admitted favourite. "But once I started in movies he and I were inseparable and there was no way she could compete or win back his full attention. Still, she tried: she laboured over the piano and took ballet. But the wounds went deep. After a few such tries he gave up on her and she felt even more rejected than before." (Cary, 1978) Although Baby Peggy realised that her sister was feeling left out, and tried to help on occasion, Louise simply felt patronised, and was routinely referred to by reporters as Baby Peggy's little sister". This scenario is typical and contains all the classic ingredients of envy, rejection and futility following unsuccessful attempts to share the limelight and the attention of the parents. Even the wills of parents sometimes reflected the most one-sided favouritism. When Mary Pickford's mother left over $3 million, $200,000 each went to Lottie, Jack and Gwynne whereas it was Mary, who needed it least, who got the remaining $2,500,000.

Another interesting example is John Wilkes Booth, who achieved notoriety by assassinating Abraham Lincoln. He was a failed actor who had lived in the shadow of his more successful brothers Edwin and Junius. To what extent this motivated the crime that made him famous is a matter for speculation. But it may be significant that his highly dramatic act took place in a theatre. The result at any rate was that he became infinitely more historically important than anyone in his family. According to Lane (1959), although he claimed to be striking a blow for 'the South' his real revenge was directed at his own family. "It was the furies of jealousy that drove the actor to fire the shot that shook the Western World."

Milgram and Ross (1982) studied 15 obscure siblings of famous people and the effects this fame had on their own development. Most attributed their sibling's fame to expertise and hard work in some field of public interest. They also stressed that the parents had been supportive of their siblings' creativity and achievement. At the same time they complained that their parents often instigated rivalry between the children, by holding up the successful sibling as a model for comparison against which the sibling who achieved less was a 'failure'. Many reported difficulties in developing an independent identity and self-respect.

Sisters of famous brothers often felt that their parents expected less of them because they were female, and this certainly held up the career of Mendelssohn's gifted sister Fanny, who languished at home while her brother Felix was taken round the European capitals and introduced to Goethe and other influential figures of the time. Felix was implacably against her having a musical career and insisted she publish her songs under his own name. A number of studies have confirmed that gifted women tend to do better when they do not have to compete for parental and other resources with talented or assertive brothers (Helson, 1990, Winner, 1996).

PARTNERS OF FAMOUS PEOPLE

It may not be wise for stage romances to happen professionally but they frequently do. For a start, fellow performers may be on a very close wavelength, and the added closeness and physical adrenaline of doing intimate scenes may trigger off a sexual buzz and tip the balance in favour of dissolving a previous relationship. Actors are thrown together on tour and in rehearsals so there is a constant physical closeness, and the 'fun together' effect can be heightened by the post performance rise in adrenaline and the elated party mood where the late night atmosphere can make things happen. Many partners lurk around the set for that reason. When the electricity really strikes, as with Richard Burton and Elizabeth Taylor during the filming of 'Cleopatra', the results can be magnetic, on screen and off. Interestingly, during the filming of 'Who's Afraid of Virginia Woolf?', the dynamic of their faltering marriage in real life was reflected through the 'spark' between them on screen.

Another reason why stage romances happen is far more mundane. Successful actors are easy targets for up and coming ones who want to further their careers. There is a definite 'scalp taking' value in sleeping with the more famous – it may increase perceived social and professional status and on a purely practical level can give access to the partner's range of contacts, party round and media presence. Relationships between producers/directors and actresses could also be cynically analysed as a trade-off between power and career prospects on the one hand and talent, youth and beauty on the other, hence the 'casting couch' phenomenon. Actors can also sleep with politicians for mutual gain, though the gain in prestige for the politician may be outweighed by the scandal if they are already married. Actors are ambitious people, and given that four out of five are unemployed at any given moment (UK Equity figures), they can go to extraordinary lengths to increase their chances of working.

FAME AND DIVORCE

"If I could live and breathe a little more lightly at times rather than be dragged down about my work, I think I'd be a better wife to someone" – thus Kim Novak (Modern Screen, November, 1961, in TTT) described the stresses that being a famous actress imposed on marriage. Another constant stress on relationships is the media. 'A and B happily married again today' is not news. 'A seen in late night spot with C; A claims we are just good friends' is news. It may be true, it may not be true, but it is constant. In one year, pop band Oasis generated a quite unbelievable number of separate news stories, through journalists parking outside Liam and Patsy Kensit's flat ready to turn almost any movement into a story. The anger of Liam and the tension on their relationship was obvious.

In the world of the beautiful people mutual attractions between stars may be as much of a marriage breaker as the stresses of fame. These may happen on tour, on or off the set, as a result of the highs of recreational drugs, or more cynically, from taking up with more exciting, influential or 'hot' people. Sometimes in marriages between people in the public eye the relationship is kept in the news by break offs, rumours of infidelity and other sensational factors. Taking cynicism one step further, one wonders if eight marriages, including remarriage to Richard Burton, had something to do with good publicity in the case of Elizabeth Taylor, who famously said at one point "My family life is more important to me than my career. How many Hollywood marriages do you know of where the wife is an actress and the marriage still works?" (McClelland, 1985) To what extent do famous actors act out their private lives? It is likely that the exhibitionist and narcissistic natures of some famous people makes them difficult if not impossible to live with. Rita Hayworth, describing her life with Orson Welles, said that "when he awoke each morning he expected her to applaud". (Hamilton, 1997)

REFERENCES

Albert, RS (1996) *What the study of excellence can teach us*, Creativity Research Journal 9, 307–315

Cary, Diana Serra (1978) *Hollywood's Children – An Inside Account* of *the Child Star Era* Dallas USA: Southern Methodist University Press.

Elias, Norbert (1993) *Mozart*, Portrait of a Genius

Hamilton, LH (1997) *The Person behind the Mask: A guide to Performing Arts Psychology* Greenwich CT, Ablex Publishing Co.

Helson, R (1990) Creativity in Women: outer and inner views over time, in Runco and Albert *Theories of Creativity* Newbury Park, CA, Sage Books

Knafo, D (1991) *Psychoanalytic Psychology* 8, 263–281

Lane, Y (1959) *The Psychology of the Actor* London, Secker and Warburg

McClelland, Doug (1985) *Hollywood on Hollywood – Tinsel Town Talks* Winchester MA USA: Faber and Faber

Milgram, JI and Ross, HG (1982) *Effects of Fame in Adult Sibling Relationships* Individual Psychology 38, 72–79

Mitchell, G and Cronson, H (1987) *The Celebrity Family: A Clinical Perspective* American Journal of Family Therapy 15, 237–241

Sloboda, J (1990) Musical Excellence – how does it develop? In Howe MJA (ed.) *Encouraging the Development of Exceptional Skills and Talent*, Leicester: British Psychological Society

Spada, J (1983) *Judy and Liza*, London, Sidgewick and Jackson

Steri, H (1990) *Mozart, or amniotic music: a psychogenealogic study*, Psychoanalyse a l'Universite 15, 107–137

Wellisch, DK (1984) *Drug problems in the wealthy and famous*, Journal of Drug Issues 14, 233–242

Winner, E (1996) *Gifted Children: Myths*

Fame

FANS AND FAN BEHAVIOUR

The word fan comes from the Latin fanaticus, meaning someone inspired to frenzy by devotion to a deity. There is indeed a certain religious fervour in the behaviour of many fans. Just as football fans worship their heroes on the pitch and perpetrate violence out of 'loyalty' to their club, so the fans of Hollywood stars and pop singers create for themselves a sense of identity out of following the movements of their idol. They attend performances, collect records, photographs and other memorabilia and meet up and talk with like-minded others. They may try to infiltrate the life of the star as much as possible, sending them gifts, attempting to engage them in correspondence or conversation, and imagining that the object of their devotion reciprocates awareness and interest. Or they may live vicariously through the star to whom they have attached themselves, fantasising at some level that they are that person, enjoying all the pleasures and privileges of their life style.

One obvious way of identifying with the idol is to try to look like them. This may be achieved by imitating their clothing, hairstyle, make-up, accent and general mode of behaviour. If the latter is somewhat anti-social (eg drug-taking or destruction of property) this can get the fan into considerable trouble. Some fans even go as far as having plastic surgery to look more like their idol (Herman, 1982). Lookalikes may make a career themselves out of imitating a famous person (eg appearing in advertisements and opening fetes), but there is a danger of over-identification, such that the imitator loses sight of who they really are. At least one 'reincarnation' of Marilyn Monroe has committed suicide, apparently in order to complete the identification with their idol. Sometimes even the stars model themselves on an idol. When Debbie Harry claimed she was a reincarnation of Marilyn Monroe, it was unclear whether she was living in fantasy or delusion.

PARASOCIAL ATTRACTION

Communication scientists describe the relationship between fans and their idols as parasocial because they occur indirectly, through mass media rather than direct experience and actual social meetings. This includes reading about them in newspapers and magazines, watching them on films or TV and by posting and visiting internet sites set up as shrines to the stars. Other sociologists call it 'quasi-friendship', because people really believe they 'know' the star. After all, they have read articles about where they live and what they like to do, even including the most intimate details of their sex lives (for example George Michael's 'cottaging' and Bill Clinton's novel use of a cigar). It is widely supposed that, even though these relationships are one-way, they partly fulfil some of the functions of real friendships, such as providing feelings of familiarity and companionship.

How do we choose our idols? Stever (1991) analysed the appeal of celebrities into four main categories: (1) perceived sex appeal (being beautiful or strong and handsome); (2) perceived competence (a talented actor, successful sports person, or powerful politician); (3) prosocial qualities (honest, hardworking and supporting charities); (4) mystique (being mysterious, shy and misunderstood). Some mixture of these qualities was found to characterise nearly all celebrities in the eyes of the public. However, in a study of 367 people attending a Michael Jackson concert and a control group of undergraduates, Stever found that only the first three of these attributes was rated higher by 'dedicated fans' than those who were 'not fans'. Mystique ratings did not distinguish the two groups. Thus, while mystique may be a factor in one's elevation to stardom (or possibly an effect of it), it does not seem particularly to attract devoted fans.

Despite the parasocial nature of the relationship, there are ways in which fans might hope to interact more directly with their idols. One such approach is to write them letters. Leets, Becker and Giles (1995) analysed 83 fan letters received by one (male) Hollywood celebrity. They found that fans wrote to this particular celebrity for three main reasons: 16% were curious and sought specific information (How many children do you have? Did you do your own stunts in your movies? How long did it take you to break into stardom?); 39% wanted to express adulation (I think you are a wonderful talented person. I am your biggest fan, I always dream of meeting you, I love you); 46% were requesting an autograph, letter or items for a fund-raiser (Could you send me an autographed photo? My wife is such a big fan we were wondering if you could make her birthday special by sending a letter or card.) Such letter-writers can usually expect some kind of response, even if it is written by a secretary and submitted for signature by the star.

Some fans get rewarded for their devotion by establishing actual social contact with their idol. Most obviously, this occurs when an idol visits or is entertained by their fan club on their travels. But some persistent fans make contact as individuals by hanging about their homes and venues. Sir Paul McCartney had a female fan who stood outside his house almost continuously for three years. As he began to feel comfortable that her presence was non-threatening he would chat with her, allow her to walk his sheepdog and even get her to open the security gates at night when he had forgotten his keys (Norman, 1981). Other pop stars use their fans as unofficial archivists, since they often have remarkable memories and documentation concerning the activities and concert itineraries of their idols. Any such interaction or concession is taken by the fan as evidence that their idol is a 'very nice person' and gives them something to boast about to their friends. The ultimate form of contact sought by many fans is of course sexual, and pop singers and football stars are particularly likely to capitalise on the sexual availability of adoring fans or groupies.

FROM HISTRIONICS TO HYSTERIA

It is quite normal for a teenager to worship an idol. The idol crystallises some important preoccupation or desire, for example a model of sporting prowess or sexual attractiveness or a focus of rebellion against parental authority. Adoration of the idol serves purposes such as goal definition and the personification of deep emergent impulses, making them more concrete and identifiable. The sexual awakenings of a young woman may take shape in the image of Leonardo DiCaprio as Romeo, while the rebellious stirrings of a young man may focus on thoughts of James Dean riding a Harley-Davidson motor cycle. Like having a crush on a favourite teacher, this is a typical teenage phenomenon and a perfectly healthy phase of development.

There are gender differences in the way that idolatry is manifested (Raviv et al, 1996). Except where sex symbols are concerned, boys use idols as goal definitions. They typically aspire to be like their hero – even to compete with him. They may follow a top footballer or heroic actor as a form of identification, but the true goal is to emulate, and perhaps ultimately supersede him. Girls are more inclined to attach themselves to famous men in the manner of devoted disciples. Their urge is to worship and serve rather than displace him, and their ultimate fantasy is to be 'swept off their feet' by his power. There is also more likely to be a social element to their idolatry. Wherever there is collective worship, such as crowds of fans screaming at airports or film premieres, females outnumber males considerably. Women are also more inclined than men to join fan clubs, swap dreams with like-minded peers, and display emotional contagion reactions such as screaming, crying and mass fainting.

Female group hysteria is often thought to have begun with The Beatles but it has been around much longer than that. Frank Sinatra had the 'bobby-soxers' swooning in the early days of his singing career. Earlier still, the composer Franz Liszt was a pop star of his generation, causing Victorian women to faint with ecstasy as he pounded the piano keys furiously, his long hair flying all about, in concerts of his own arrangements. Nor did the pop guru phenomenon begin with Liszt; Nicolo Paganini, the virtuoso violinist, and the prolific composer Antonio Vivaldi, known familiarly as 'The Red Priest' by virtue of his striking red mane, were prompting attacks of 'the vapours' around the turn of the 18th century. Although it may be hard for modern audiences to imagine Vivaldi sparking histrionics in teenage girls, some hint of this effect has been revived by the popularity of the street-credible violinist Nigel Kennedy's performances of 'The Four Seasons'.

Rather than simply admiring a model whom they seek to imitate, girls tend to seek shamans – all powerful magicians (gurus) who claim privileged access to the secrets of life and who demand unquestioning devotion. In this sense, pop stars are equivalent to evangelists; both often wear white suits, make theatrical use of music, lights and props, and maximise suggestibility in their public performances. It is this element of emotional engagement and semi-hypnotic absorption, which psychologists refer to as a capacity for dissociation, that seems closer to the female psyche than that of males. With the dance phenomena of the 1990s, DJs have taken on the shaman role and rave parties a certain ritualistic nature.

An interesting form of dissociation called the ("Reidentification Syndrome") consists of a tendency to confuse dramatic fiction with reality. Fulton et al (1990) describe three cases, all in elderly women. In one, an 80 year-old woman living alone repeatedly claimed to be entertaining guests who were actually participants in TV debates. Another elderly woman maintained that hospital staff were calling her names, but she was taking her material from a hospital series on the TV. The third case was that of a 90 year-old woman with progressive dementia. She thought that her grandson was being led astray by prostitutes, her son-in-law was facing charges of assault, the geriatrician in charge of her case was indulging in transvestism and a ward sister was moonlighting as a stripper. Again, these were all scenarios taken from popular TV serials with the behaviour of the fictional characters transposed onto real individuals well known to the patient. The time lag between the TV programme and the 'reidentification' was only a few hours but very persistent. Although these are extreme examples connected with dementia, many people have some capacity to let theatrical drama seep through to their everyday life, and such confusion or exaggerated fantasy may be part of the dynamics of obsessional fan attachments. Soap stars report that many people in the street believe they really are the character they portray; some have even been assaulted by members of the public who were angry with the way their character had recently behaved in the series.

FAN AND SUPERFAN

What sort of people become the most ardent fans? Stever (1995) studied "Star Trekkies" and members of rock star fan clubs using The Myers-Briggs Type Indicator (see Chapter 5). He found that "introverts" and "intuitives" were more likely to participate in fan subcultures than "extraverts" and "sensing" individuals. This indicates that an active mental (fantasy) life is more of a key to fan attachment than the social contact that might be provided by attending meetings. And if the members of fan clubs are introvert, then individual fans would almost certainly be more so.

This image of the serious fan as introverted rather than sociable and outgoing is supported by music journalist Philip Norman who visited many of them in the course of writing several pop-star biographies. He describes them as usually quiet, neat, unassuming and gentle, with prodigious memories for any fact concerning their idols. He felt that, for the most part, they were not only harmless but even to be envied. "Worshipping at their alters, they experience a happiness unavailable to the critical mind. Looking up to a myth, they can never be disillusioned. Their bedroom shrines and posters seemingly compensate for any amount of everyday boredom." (The Sunday Times, May 24, 1992).

There is a suggestion here that fan attachment is a form of defence mechanism - a way of compensating for low self-esteem, of forestalling loneliness while opting out of the disappointments that are bound to accompany real relationships. The function of idolisation in adolescent girls is to create a bridge between sexual fantasy and real sexual development. For the individual who is shy, and introvert, perhaps feeling slightly inadequate and lacking the confidence to form meaningful friendships, attachment to an idol may be quite adaptive. There is experimental evidence to suggest that the pain of personal failure can be offset by basking in the reflected glory of sports stars (Lee, 1985). Idolisation can even be viewed as a kind of secular religion with all the mental comforts that implies. According to an analysis of "Presleymania" by Olson and Crase (1990), Elvis was "a catalyst for a worldwide youth movement, a paradox of sexuality and spirituality that continues to challenge new generations and a symbol of hope for those less fortunate who shared his poor, Southern heritage".

Taking the religion analogy one step further, Conrad (1987) has suggested that idols may, effectively, be sacrificed by their fans in a semi-religious sense. He points out that people have proved, through time, a fundamental human need to sacrifice that which is dear to them in order to exorcise demons and placate deities. He then identifies a parallel in events surrounding the lives of Marilyn Monroe, Elvis Presley and Maria Callas. Each of them acquired an extremely demanding and claustrophobic following with which they seemed ill-equipped to cope, and their lives and identities were taken over to such an extent that they were driven to an early death. After that, their status as cult figures was consolidated by fans worshipping the places where they lived, the celebration of anniversaries, trading of relics, and attempts at reincarnation. James Dean, Princess Grace of Monaco and Diana, Princess of Wales, are others who seem to fit this pattern of public hounding, premature death and a kind of immortality. Conrad's analysis, with its implied continuity between sacrificial sheep and goats, the life of Christ and that of certain modern stars may seem slightly fanciful. Nevertheless, it is true that celebrities can be overwhelmed by the degree of public attention they receive, (especially since there are often malevolent components intermingled with the adulation) and a premature death certainly increases the likelihood of canonisation.

Women are particularly attracted to famous men. A recent study comparing the sexual fantasies of men and women found that whereas men were obsessed with young, shapely anonymous women, women were more inclined to fantasise about identifiable, famous men (Wilson, 1997). And such is the power of fame to attract women, that even serial killers have their groupies. Ted Bundy, who was believed to have murdered up to 100 women around his home town of Tacoma, had proposals of marriage from women all over the world while he was awaiting execution. Another example is Peter Sutcliffe, the "Yorkshire Ripper". Although declared a dangerous psychopath, Sutcliffe had several women (whom he had not previously known) fighting with each over visiting rights. The authorities at the hospital for the criminally insane to which he had been committed were understandably loath to grant visiting rights to his fans because they regarded their motives as suspect. Partly, it appeared, they were fascinated by the 'macho aura' surrounding a man capable of such atrocities; here was a man who was prepared to do exactly what he wanted regardless of the conse-quences. However, his notoriety was also a form of fame that attracted women, some of whom may have been seeking to share it. One of Sutcliffe's admirers did gain exposure in her own right, selling her story to tabloid newspapers and appearing on TV chat shows.

Not surprisingly, the type of performer or celebrity to whom one becomes attached gives clues as to one's own personality disposition. Hansen and Hansen (1991) studied fans of punk and heavy metal rock music in relation to non-fans and found that they were clearly distin-guishable. Heavy metal fans tended to be Machiavellian and macho and lower in 'need for cognition' than non-fans. They also tended to make higher estimates of the prevalence of sexual, drug-related, occult, and anti-social behaviours of young people in general. Punk rock fans were less accepting of authority than those who disliked this music and estimated higher frequencies of anti-authority types of behaviour such as owning weapons, committing crime, shoplifting and going to jail. Since estimates of behaviour are based upon experience of oneself and friends, this probably gives an indication of the life styles that are associated with these musical preferences. Consistent evidence of high levels of interest in rock music, and particularly destructive themes such as murder, suicide and satanic practices have been observed in young offenders (Wass et al, 1991).

What makes idolatry abnormal is probably just a matter of degree. If it carries on into the mature years, becoming a substitute for inti-mate contact that interferes with friendship and marriage, if it is so obsessional that work and day-to-day life is disrupted, if there is detachment from reality to a degree that is delusional, and if the safety of the fan themselves or others is jeopardised, then it may be a matter for clinical concern.

At the harmless end are members of fan clubs who enjoy each other's company and have outings together. For example, the 1970s TV series 'The Professionals' has an active fan club some 20 years after being taken off the air. "We have watched the show hundreds of times. Loads of us go to Blackpool for a Professionals day out and we have special Professionals T-shirts printed with 'They're Hard' written on them. We have a glove puppet and a big black curly wig that we take with us and go up to strangers, make them wear the wig and have their picture taken with the puppet. We have a big board of these photos now. We have met up with a lot of other Professionals fans along the way." (TV documentary 'Dating the Enemy', Lifetime Productions, 1997). This group of about 12 women and 2 men appeared fairly light-hearted about their devotion to their heroes, tough guy cops Bodie and Doyle (a sort of British Starsky and Hutch) and use them as a focus for sociable occasions.

Isolated fans are more likely to appear abnormal, although even here some adaptive aspects of the behaviour can be identified. One woman was so obsessed with country singer Jim Reeves that she made her husband change his name to Jim. Although seemingly eccentric, this was reasonably well tolerated by her husband and led to her appearing on several chat-shows and becoming a mini-celebrity in her own right. Madonna's 'No1 fan', Michelle Budd, has also done the rounds of newspaper, magazine and TV appearances, but at a greater price in terms of disruption to her life. According to her own account, she quit jobs in order to be closer to Madonna, walked out of hospital too soon after a serious operation hoping to catch a glimpse of her. Besotted with Madonna for 17 years, she spent her last £100 bribing a security man to get access to a studio where Madonna was performing, and no longer speaks to her family because "they are religious and think Madonna is the Devil". Every night she goes out to clubs that she believes Madonna might visit, in the hope of meeting her. "I would love to go to bed with Madonna but have accepted this will never happen; I haven't been able to find anyone to have an intimate relationship with because Madonna is too important." ('Dating the Enemy').

Other fan attachments are even more clearly self-destructive. A 24 year old woman from Leicestershire fell in love with Michael Jackson when she was ten and followed him for 12 years hoping that he would be the first man she ever kissed. She spent £10,000 attending 120 of his concerts and developed anorexia and other illnesses similar to whatever sickness Jackson was reported as having at the time. When "Jacko" was accused of child-molestation by a teenage boy, the woman was so incensed that she threatened to kill the accuser and was consequently sent to a high security prison in Los Angeles (Daily Star, 11/4/94). Having devoted herself to Jackson for so long she apparently could not accept this assault on his integrity and felt compelled to avenge him. This illustrates the extremes to which an obsession may be taken.

BEWARE GEEKS BEARING GIFTS

Fans can be dangerous in various ways. Excessive enthusiasm and the desire to get close and touch the object of devotion can be a problem even in the absence of any malicious intent. Stars are often mobbed to such a degree that the sheer pressure of bodies jostling to see or get near them can physically injure them. At the height of their fame in San Francisco, The Beatles had to be escorted from their plane in a protective steel cage to prevent them being crushed by the adoring crowds (Norman, 1981). And even if the stars themselves are unharmed, unruly crowd behaviour can be a problem, particularly with rock events. Led Zeppelin concerts, for example, were frequently disrupted by audience violence. On one occasion the police in Milan were involved in a pitched battle with 15,000 fans (Welch, 1984). At a concert given by The Who in Cincinnati in 1979, eleven people were crushed to death in a rush to obtain seats close to the stage (Herman, 1982). Such incidents are not unique to rock concerts, but this kind of music seems to arouse passions more than most.

The groupies who hang about stage doors and cast parties hoping not just to meet, but also have sex with their idol may also represent a danger to a star. Whether or not intended at the outset, these encounters often lead to 'kiss-and-tell' stories being sold to tabloid newspapers, with consequences that vary from enhancement of the idol's reputation to devastation of their private life and career. High libido stars such as Rod Stewart and Mick Jagger walk a tightrope, caught in conflict between their immediate sexual desires and the threat of marital disruption with the likelihood of highly expensive and messy divorce proceedings. High profile politicians are equally prey to groupies. The Monica Lewinsky affair that embroiled Bill Clinton is a famous case in point, even though it may not have been Monica herself but political opponents and opportunists who initiated all the damaging publicity.

Perhaps the most dangerous fans of all are those who become persistent stalkers. This behaviour may begin out of apparent admiration but the individuals concerned often have such fragile self-esteem and such a tenuous grip on reality that any imagined slight (even though their idol may be barely aware of their existence) may be enough to trigger lethal hostility. Actress Rebecca Schaeffer, who starred in Woody Allen's film 'Radio Days', was shot dead on her own doorstep by a deranged fanatic who had been following her about for some time and took exception to her refusing to accept his gift of a huge teddy bear. The passion that motivates the pursuit can quickly and easily turn from adoration to hate in individuals who are mentally unstable. A great many modern celebrities are bothered by stalkers at some time or another in their careers and need to have bodyguards to protect them from variously motivated weirdos. Lauren Bacall, Nyree Dawn Porter, Diana Rigg, Olivia Newton-John, Sheena Easton and Cher are among the female stars who have reported to have been tormented by stalkers.

The behaviours exhibited by stalkers are variable, ranging from persistent following of a threatening nature (eg hiding in shadows outside the home of their victim), obscene phone calls and letters, the sending of unnerving gifts (such as wrapped faeces or voodoo dolls pierced through the heart) to actual physical attacks. Their motivation is equally variable. Sometimes they are just obsessed by their targets and engaging in a kind of addictive behaviour. A major reinforcement is often the sense of potency or self-importance that is gained (albeit through such a remote association with a celebrity). Sometimes they are suffering psychotic delusions that may involve some convoluted logic, for example 'my mother deserted me at an early age; this person reminds me of my mother and I will not let her escape so easily'. The ghastly slaughter of the pregnant actress Sharon Tate and her friends in 1969, by Charles Manson's hippy family, was supposedly in obedi-

ence to the lyrics of two Beatle songs - though it could also be inter-
preted as extreme envy of their Bel Air lifestyle (the word "pigs" was
daubed in blood at the crime scene). Clearly, many stalkers are psychologically unstable, or even insane, and perhaps more in need of
treatment than punishment, but this does not make them any less
dangerous to their victims.

Some stalkers suffer from a pathological love condition called eroto-
mania (sometimes called De Clerambeault's Syndrome, after the French
doctor who identified it in 1942). Such individuals, who may be male
or female, are seriously deluded, somehow becoming convinced without evidence, that their victim is really in love with them but is
prevented from reciprocating because of circumstances (because they
are married, or do not wish to jeopardise their career and so on). The
person they hanker for is normally out of their reach in social terms
(usually a top professional such as a professor, doctor or lawyer or a
film star), yet they convince themselves that they are being sent secret
love messages, such as wearing a tie in their favourite colour or incor-
porating cryptic lyrics in their songs. Helena Bonham Carter was
pursued for six years by a young man who bombarded her with letters
and phone calls before being served with a court injunction banning
him from going anywhere near her. Undaunted, he told The Sun newspaper, "I still care for her and feel she'd like to speak to me". Skating
star Katarina Witt was stalked for two years by an erotomaniac who
followed her around on her world tours and sent threatening letters,
one of which read: "Please don't be afraid when God allows me to pull
you out of your boots to hold you tight. Then you'll know there is life
beyond the flesh". In 1982, actress Theresa Saldana suffered a near
fatal stabbing from a fan who claimed that God wanted them "united in
heaven".

Not all attackers of celebrities are motivated by frustration at being
denied a relationship with their idol. Sometimes, it seems, they simply
want to share the fame of the target (Sargent, 1975). Mark Chapman,
who shot John Lennon outside his New York apartment in 1980, was
apparently so obsessed with his idol that he wanted his name to go
down beside that of Lennon for posterity. It is sobering to reflect that
he pretty much succeeded in this aim. A number of other celebrities
have apparently been assassinated just so that people will sit up and
take notice of an individual who otherwise might have gone through

life as a nobody. An attempt on the life of Ronald Reagan, whilst he was President, was apparently carried out in order to impress Jodie Foster. The gay serial killer Andrew Cunanan, had worked his way up a scale of lesser public figures before ensuring his notoriety by murdering Gianni Versace, the world-famous designer, at South Beach, Florida. Perhaps Cunanan had taken note of the fact that while Presidents Lincoln and Kennedy are remembered with affection, the names of John Wilkes Booth and Lee Harvey Oswald (their assassins) have not been forgotten either. It is a chilling irony that Cunanan's classmates at his school graduation voted him the man "Most Likely to be Remembered".

Whatever the motives of those who stalk the stars, life as a top celebrity has now become so dangerous that nearly all of them now need to be constantly protected by body guards of the kind previously associated with Mafia bosses (cf the film 'The Bodyguard'). This applies not just to beautiful young starlets who might risk sexual molestation, and politicians who inevitably have enemies, but even film tough guys like Sylvester Stallone and strapping male sports stars such as Mike Tyson and Tiger Woods. The concern is that some madman (or woman) may see them as trophies for conquest. Tiger Woods is provided with an armed escort whenever he plays golf tournaments, especially since a persistent heckler restrained by police was found to be carrying a gun. Hollywood now has security firms that specialise in threat assessment and management and there is a Los Angeles police unit dealing specifically with stalkers. These units sift thousands of sinister letters and phone-calls every year and take appropriate action. It is estimated that about one in ten of the perpetrators are likely ultimately to confront their target in person.

SUITABLE CASES FOR TREATMENT

Leets et al (1995) discuss the differences between normal fans and those who are threatening. Both express a desire for contact with the celebrity but the inappropriate and dangerous pursuers studied by Dietz et al (1991) have unreasonable and bizarre expectations; requesting valuable gifts, marriage, sex or having children with their idol. However, the difficulty in distinguishing clearly between normal and dangerous fans is highlighted by an interview with a particular fan called Brenda. Brenda remarked that she and her celebrity were "meant to be together". In her ideal world, she hoped that after meeting and talking with him he would fall in love with her and slip on the wedding ring. She also claimed that she was willing to "do something wild and crazy to get his attention". These wild fantasies were interspersed with more grounded comments such as "of course, I may not actually get to meet him" and "he may not be nice". Once she learned that he was engaged her infatuation subsided greatly. Leets et al suggest that it is these reality checks (the capacity to recognise fantasy for what it is) that separate the normal from the pathological fan.

What sorts of treatments are available for stalking and obsessive fan behaviour? The first problem is to convince the individual that they need help and this is particularly difficult with those who are psychotically deluded. In such cases, treatment may only be possible with a court order or psychiatric commitment of some kind and anti-psychotic medication may be required. This may be done in hospital, but with the current emphasis on care in the community, a care worker may be assigned to supervise administration of the drug. In the absence of such treatment, which at times can be remarkably effective, it may be necessary to send a dangerous stalker to prison to protect their victim, as in the case of Denise Pfeiffer, Michael Jackson's tormentor.

In less severe, non-psychotic conditions, a drug such as Prozac (which enhances self-control by raising levels of a brain chemical called serotonin) could be helpful. However, cognitive-behaviour therapy administered by a qualified clinical psychologist is the preferred treatment because it seeks to give clients control over their own behaviour without dependence on any drug at all. The main principles are: (1) working on the beliefs and attitudes that sustain the irrational behaviour, if possible exposing them as fallacious and restructuring them in more positive ways; (2) building self-esteem so that the client feels better equipped for developing rewarding relationships among their peers – attachments that are concrete rather than fantasy based; (3) learning a technique called "thought stopping", whereby obsessional thoughts are identified and a procedure for over-riding them with more constructive ideas and activities is put in place; (4) homework exercises that offer distraction from the obsession by building alternative sources of reward.

The precise details of these programmes are flexible and depend upon the particular circumstances of the client. They are worked out together with the therapist as agreed aims. Modern psychological therapy pays minimal attention to the presumed childhood origins of a problem and tends to focus on altering behaviour in the here-and-now in an up-front manner. Such methods are proving to be very effective.

REFERENCES

Conrad, P (1987) *A Song of Death: The Meaning of Opera*. London: Chatto and Windus.

Dietz, PE, Matthews, DB, Van Duyne, et al (1991) *Threatening and otherwise inappropriate letters to Hollywood celebrities*. Journal of Forensic Sciences, 36, 185–209.

Fulton, JD, MacDonald, E And Scott, PJ (1990) *Television: Fantastic reality or realistic fantasy?* Journal of the American Geriatrics Society , 38, 829.

Hansen, CH, and Hansen, RD (1991) *Constructing personality and social reality through music: Individual differences among fans of punk and heavy metal music*. Journal of broadcasting and Electronic Media. 35, 335–350.

Herman, G (1982) *Rock'n'Roll Babylon*. London: Plexus.

Lee, MJ (1985) *Self-esteem and social identity in basketball fans: A closer look at basking in reflected glory*. Journal of Sport Behaviour, 8, 210–223.

Leet, L, De Becker, G, and Giles, H (1995) *Fans: Exploring expressed motivations for contacting celebrities*. Journal of Language and Social Psychology, 14, 102–123.

Norman, P. (1981) *Shout! The True Story of The Beatles*. London: Hamish Hamilton.

Olson, M, Crase, D (1990) *Presleymania: The Elvis factor*. Death Studies, 14, 277–282.

Raviv, A, Bar-Tal, D, Raviv, A and Ben-Horin, A (1996) *Adolescent idolisation of pop singers: Causes, expressions and reliance*. Journal of Youth and Adolescence. 25, 631–650.

Sargent, DA (1975) *A contribution to the study of the presidential assassination syndrome*. Adolescent Psychiatry 4, 299–308.

Stever, GS (1991) *The Celebrity Appeal Questionnaire*. Psychological Reports, 68, 859–866.

Stever, GS (1995) *Gender by type interaction effects in mass media subcultures*. Journal of Psychological Type, 32, 3–22.

Wass, HM, Miller, MD, and Redditt, CA (1991) *Adolescents and destructive themes in rock music: A follow-up*. Omega: Journal of Death and Dying, 23, 199–206.

Welch, C (1984) *Led Zeppelin: The Book*. London: Proteus Books.

Wilson, GD (1997) *Gender differences in sexual fantasy: An evolutionary analysis*. Personality and Individual Differences, 22, 27–31.

Fame

THE SOCIAL CONTEXT OF FAME

Famous people have always tended to share their social world with other famous people. For a start, there are frequently opportunities to hustle for more business, to do some useful networking, or to flirt with potentially powerful or useful people. They may be able to relax more, being among equals rather than fans who will relate to the image more than the real person. Equal status may also apply to money, thus keeping gold diggers away. Frequently 'In' groups of famous people – such as pop stars or actors – share common interests, mutual friends and a similar sense of humour, so socialising is also a way of keeping in touch with developments and being on the same wavelength. Cross-mix groups of famous people are also rewarding, since besides the communality of fame there are also the different fields in which it is won – showbiz, sport, politics. Hobbies mix in an active way with careers – pop stars like Rod Stewart and Elton John are active in the football world, and many celebrities and other sportspeople play organised golf tournaments. The apotheosis of the social world of fame is the big 'set pieces' – the political elections, the Rock Festivals, the international charity appeals and the Oscars, where celebrities of all kinds indulge in self-promotion, creating a galaxy of egos all trying to outshine each other.

This phenomenon is seen all over the world at showbiz parties, fashionable restaurants and holiday resorts, premieres and political and sporting events. But perhaps nowhere in the history of fame have so many famous people lived in one place, as happened when the movie industry centred its activities on the little town of Hollywood – a suburb of Los Angeles – looking for a good climate and a variety of available outdoor scenery. The social psychology generated in that one place has filled many a bookshelf – not least with the memoirs of nearly all the stars who experienced it in its heyday.

ON HOLLYWOOD TIME

"Peel away the phony tinsel in Hollywood and you find the real tinsel." (Oscar Levant, in McClelland, 1986).

'Hollywood time' is a phrase used to describe that particular superficiality of a social world, where an omnipresent and hyper-friendly façade in the people you meet covers up a ruthlessly manipulative internal need for power, money and advancement. It may conceal a lot more, since there is a fair share of personality problems, aggression,

Fame

addictions and other personal troubles. In this 'Hello-Goodbye' world "Where are you?" (Where are you working?) is more important than "How are you?", and the bottom line is utility. People of the moment are useful introductions to parties, agents, executives, actors and the chance of work, so personal contacts are filtered quickly and ended when there appears to be no benefit in continuing them, so enabling the social prowl to resume.

People have their own agendas which they hustle day in and day out, because in the transitory world of showbusiness every step up the ladder means more money, more power, and the greatest thing of all – more control. More control means moving a step closer to decision making, cutting better deals, getting bigger parts and ultimately getting more percentage of production revenues. All of these act as a buffer against the fickleness of showbiz fashion and allow for a chance to invest money and guarantee the future against poverty and unemployment. The main goal in LA is work. In that sense, it is an actors town – people are always name dropping and trying to get noticed. Equally the writers and all the other associated freelancers are looking for opportunities, trying to make that magic connection in any way possible, even by very long chains of contacts. Work is the golden key to having your own career, your own contracts, your own security and your own name in lights. Progress is moving from a bit part or being a backing singer to a main part or lead singer. Vonda Shepard, previously in demand as a backing singer with Jackson Browne and others, got her big break when she won the music deal for the Ally McBeal show, in which she sings, writes and occasionally performs.

The legendary 'friendliness' of Hollywood is, in reality, only friendly according to status. The hierarchical nature of Hollywood was well expressed by Jean-Pierre Aument: "Hollywood was rigidly stratified. Every night there were the $10,000 a week parties where nobody who made under $8,000 was invited. Then there were the $5,000 parties, the $2,000 parties and so on." (Aument, 1997) The simplest division used was the A Group – the top producers, directors and stars – and the B Group which contained all the rest, and was subdivided into those with lead parts, those with a few lines, stunt men, extras and so on down. On top of that, day by day status shifts divided the A Group into those who were 'hot' (working on current big movies) and those who were 'cool' (idle at the time). As Peter Strauss said, "Your worth in this town is determined by your degree of success. It's a horrible fact. You make the party list once you are in the limelight and you are recognisable. You know the next question is going to be 'What are you doing now?'" (Rhona Barrett's Hollywood, the 1970s, in McClellend, 1985). For that reason, those who were not working were simply not invited to parties, nor would they want to go to them and be subjected to embarrassing questions.

THE BEAUTIFUL PEOPLE

Hollywood is the capital of plastic surgery. Even in its early days, the first place a newly signed star went to was the dentist in order to get a perfect set of white teeth, even before the makeover and the new name. As Ann Todd said: "Glamour was the magic word. Everything had to be geared to what the producers thought the public imagined was the perfect romantic male or ideal woman. If one of your eyebrows didn't match the other it had to be made identical. If your mouth was crooked, that had to be made straight. If you had no bust, they gave you one. Rotten teeth – they whipped them out." (Todd, 1980) Clint Eastwood tells the same story: "For years I bummed around trying to get a job. It was same old story. My voice was too soft, my teeth needed capping, I squinted too much, I was too tall. And I know that if I walked into a casting office right now and nobody knew I was Clint Eastwood, I would get the same old treatment." (McClellend, 1985)

Psychology works on the side of the casting agencies here – there is ample evidence from psychological studies that physical beauty leads people to overrate the ability and personality of people judged on photographs alone. Psychologist Dr Nancy Etcoff underlines previous research that mothers are more likely to talk to and play with beautiful babies, three month old babies stare longest at attractive people when shown pictures, and teachers expect good looking pupils to be smarter and more sociable. It even confirms the benefits of 'symmetry', quoting research that people with symmetrical appearances are regarded as more attractive than those with irregular features, and also that symmetry is a sign of health and longevity (Etcoff, 1999).

Medical makeovers have increased steadily in sophistication as collagen and silicone fill the parts science previously could not reach. But even without the surgeon's knife beauty is everywhere, both male

Fame

and female. Even the dogs and cats are beautiful. Beauty means temptation, hence the legendary flirting and the predatory attacks on anyone useful, rich or powerful. It is not the environment for keeping relationships together.

MONEY IS KING

From the beginning, Hollywood has had a reputation of being money mad, and treating everything and everyone as a commodity. As Diana Serra Cary puts it in 'Hollywood's Children': "In sharp contrast to the dynastic, structured theatre world, the Hollywood of 1918 was nearly as wide open as any gold camp. Social elites were never honoured by the motion picture people who flocked there after 1912. Money substituted for good family and 'stardom' covered a multitude of sins. While other newcomers to Beverly Hills might have mistaken it for a high-class neighbourhood, Charlotte Pickford (mother of Mary Pickford) recognised it for what it really was – the fish market all over again. Not only objects but people were evaluated in terms of how much they cost." (Cary, 1978)

Boller and Davis (1987) recount how it all began: "Most of the studio heads were immigrants. They came from varied backgrounds, but nearly all had been poor and practically all were Jewish, willing to enter an industry not yet respectable. Carl Laemmle, the tenth of thirteen children, emigrated from Germany and had been in the clothing business. Adolph Zukor, orphaned as a boy in Hungary, became a furrier's apprentice shortly after coming to America. Samuel Goldfish (later Goldwyn) had been an office boy in Poland, then a blacksmith's assistant, and eventually went into the glove business in America. Louis B. Mayer came from Russia and worked in scrap metal before setting up his own junk business. Later Mayer claimed he could remember nothing of his Russian boyhood except hunger. The father of the Warner Brothers was a cobbler from the Polish village of Kraznashiltz, who travelled as a peddler before settling with his family in Youngstown, Ohio, where son Jack worked in a meat market."

At its worst, the market town reality has been well expressed by humorist and screen writer SJ Perelman: "Hollywood is a dreary industrial town controlled by hoodlums of enormous wealth, the ethereal sense of a pack of jackals and taste so degraded that it befouled everything it touched." (The 30's, in McClelland, 1986). Marilyn Monroe herself complained that none of the wealth was ploughed back into the social life of the city, making it little more than a film set: "If you've noticed in Hollywood where millions and billions of dollars have been made, there aren't any kind of monuments or museums. Nobody left anything behind, they grabbed it and ran – the ones who made the billions, never the workers." ('In her own words', 1983).

HOLLYWOOD'S MADNESS

Hollywood's distortion of reality into fantasy affected people in different ways, depending largely on whether they were happier in real time or on Hollywood time. Many people expressed in different ways the fact that the town could distort reality. "Hollywood is dangerous. It can warp your point of view so easily. I wonder how players and writers and directors can go on out there, year after year, and expect to keep their balance. They can't, of course", was how Paul Muni saw it (American Theatre Magazine, 1940). One solution was to stay out of it as much as possible. Montgomery Clift tried (unsuccessfully) to avoid its claws: "I prefer living in New York instead of Hollywood. Out there you start out with your own ideas but then you find yourself going the next guy's way. Before you know it you don't know what you think or want, or what you believe in." Montgomery Clift, June 1949, McClelland, 1985).

Many of the more aware people in Hollywood found its superficiality tiring, and its insularity from the true import of world events intellectually disturbing. "I detested Hollywood from the moment I arrived. Most of my friends were writers – they were the only people I wanted to be with even though in Hollywood they're rated as third-class citizens", was how Geraldine Fitzgerald experienced it. (It was fun while it lasted, 1973, McClelland, 1985).

In a town which takes its 'reality' not from the world but from the film industry, some, including director John Boorman, could find it fundamentally spooky and unnerving. "The back lots of the studios with their Western streets, their New York brownstones, Middle American main street, seem more solid than the suburbs surrounding them. As reality slips away and unbearable lightness takes hold, you must hurry into a movie theatre and connect with a film. In LA the shadows are more real than the substance." (Kent, 1991) Or as Brandon de Wilde put it: "Hollywood's a funny place. The people are very strange. They all seem to have fronts and no backs. They're just like the sets." (Motion Picture, April, 1953).

In this inverted reality, as in the film 'The Unbearable Lightness of Being', people may prefer to live within the bubble rather than outside it. "Hollywood people are afraid to leave Hollywood. Out in the world they are frightened. They are unsure of themselves. They never enjoy themselves," said producer Gottfried Reinhardt. (Kent, 1991) This view was echoed by Powdermaker: "Most of the inhabitants seem to enjoy and receive a certain security from being only with people like themselves. Members of a Melanesian tribe in the South-West Pacific likewise cannot imagine living anywhere else and are fearful of going beyond their own small community." (Powdermaker, 1950)

What can we learn from the Hollywood heyday continued after the war. But by the late fifties and sixties, Hollywood had quietened down significantly – big parties were rare, and the 'colony' atmosphere had changed into a production line of bulk lower cost productions, more for TV than film. To the nostalgic few, this was a change for the worse. For everyone else it was a breath of fresh air, though the obsession with money continued seamlessly through all transformations. So did the tradition of sticking with accepted values. When it was politically correct to show women in high places we had women as judges, doctors, politicians, even as captain of the Starship Enterprise. The trend to depict tough women resulted in their wearing guns, doing karate and fighting aliens. When it was politically correct to show blacks outwitting whites, films such as 'In the Heat of the Night' and 'Guess Who's Coming to Dinner' were made. Later, Native Americans received significant exposure in 'A Man Called Horse' and 'Dances with Wolves'. Hollywood stayed in the mainstream – it did not tread on the wrong feet because it knew where the economic power lay.

The key feature of Hollywood is not glamour. Hollywood sells glamour. The key feature is merchandising of product. Because people are the product, and the people are largely actors, the social environment is not unlike a constant casting session, with prospective stars jostling for position, saying their lines and carrying out their business during the day and partying at night. The fact that Hollywood values influenced generations across the entire world should not delude people into thinking that as a whole they were based on any real depth. In its heyday Hollywood turned out A movies in a month and B movies in nine days. Shooting started at nine in the morning, day in and day out. Nor were values based on humanity or ethics, any more than politics is. As Fred Allen put it, "All the sincerity in Hollywood you can stuff in a flea's navel and still have room for four caraway seeds and an agent's heart." (McClelland, 1985)

Hollywood's values were expedient and subservient at any period in its history to what sold tickets. Its values could also be quite contradictory, combining prudishness with an obsession for including sexual interest and images. As Claude Binion remarked: "Hollywood must never permit censorship to collapse – it's far too good for the box office." (McClelland, 1985) Hollywood's saving grace was that with the money it had at its disposal it could buy the best. Outside the studios were the gleaming rows of custom built automobiles. Inside, were some of the best creative artists the cinema has ever known. What Hollywood actually did with that constellation of talent is something for sociologists and media studies academics to debate for a long time into the future.

HOLLYWOOD VERSUS OTHER 'STAR ENVIRONMENTS'

Hollywood is an actor's town. Actors act; that is they play roles which differ from reality in various key respects. Their distortions may be about age, beauty, status and romance. A similar star environment with distortions and role play is in the world of politics – except in that world they call it 'spin'. If we examine Washington and Capitol Hill (and no doubt Brussels) we would expect to see the same public face on proceedings as we would find amongst the sets of Tinsel Town. The media image of politicians contains the same physical makeovers – the perfect teeth, the smiles, the dyed hair and the hairpieces, the photo opportunities. The media image of their political statements contains the selectivity, evasiveness and spin that constitute its 'truth makeover'.

Washington and Hollywood seem fascinated by each other, and have much in common. Washington, like Hollywood, is a financially speculative marketplace full of gamblers, an ephemeral world where fame is short lived. Hence the frenzy of enormous personal ambition, and the interpersonal encounters calculated to achieve actual personal goals as fast as possible rather than simply pass the time pleasantly or deepen friendships. Intimacy is not the goal – at mealtimes the most crowded restaurants are chosen, and you don't just network, you table hop. In any case, people using each other would destroy intimacy. The definition of a 'game' in Transactional Analysis (a systematic theory of explaining human behaviour as 'transactions' devised by psychologist Eric Berne, and called TA for short) is a set of actions and behaviour which 'destroys intimacy', and in this sense both environments are 'gamey'. This is the very word used by Hortense Powdermaker in 'The Dream Factory': "It takes all the running you can do to stay in the same place. Always there is that struggle for more and more of something, whether money, prestige, power, sensations, or what not, until the man drops dead. The game becomes the end and is played compulsively." (Powdermaker, 1950) Compulsive repetition is another of the parameters by which Berne defines a 'game'. (Berne, 1964)

What is unnerving for the public at large – in the wider world as well as the US – is that between them these two micro-environments shape the macro media and political environments we all have to live in. Given the lack of human intimacy and obsession with power and money of both Hollywood and Washington, what hope is there for deeper values in a world created by the gods of spin? Or as Hollywood calls it 'leverage' – "the ability to control a person or situation to your own advantage" (Kent, 1991), which is itself driven by higher forces than money itself – fame, success and the desire to always be a winner.

The popular music world is different in many key respects. It is more co-operative – the score for team values in the 16 Personality Factor Questionnaire (a psychometric test devised by psychologist Raymond Cattell to describe 16 basic human personality traits) is positive, and the Belbin 'Team' role score (derived from the eight main roles played within organisations) is similar to the population average (Evans 1994). Musicians do not need direction or production to perform as in the case of actors and they do not rely on being elected in order to perform like politicians. A well-known musician can go to any night spot and be asked to sit in spontaneously, which is one of the joys of the common language of music. Also, partly because of the spontaneous nature of music making, the people in it are more genuine, scoring as "forthright" on the 16PF factor N, rather than shrewd or Machiavellian (Evans, 1994). This includes well-known musicians, who were similar on this factor to lesser known ones. Arts and media counsellors like Andy Evans and Catherine Butler have noted that musicians tend to be more comfortable using 'natural' client-centred methods of therapy (straight talking and equal status of both parties) rather than 'psychoanalytical' ones – where the analyst and analysand are playing roles required by the transference phenomenon (no self disclosure or socialising by the analyst).

Musicians also use a non-verbal means of communication in their work, and so when not working tend to use verbal communication both to relax and create intimacy and to 'perform' by telling endless jokes, many of them 'insider' jokes largely incomprehensible to outsiders. This alternative or lateral style of communication may be partly to do with the right-brained predominance of music as a sound medium, as opposed to the left-brained predominance of verbal analysis, though professional classical musicians showed more left-brained response while actually listening to music than non-professionals did (Shuter-Dyson and Gabriel, 1981). Music itself has an enhancing effect on mood, demonstrated through its use in Music Therapy. It may even have bene-ficial effects on the working of the brain, if we are to believe the ongoing studies into the effect of Mozart on IQ scores, and also on the human immune system (Bartlett et al, 1993).

Consequently, one would expect star environments of musicians to be less artificial. Where such environments exist – Nashville, the coun-try and western and more recently the new popular music studio capital of the US, and the occasional rock 'super' concert (Woodstock, Live Aid) – the atmosphere of friendliness, genuineness and co-opera-tion is very evident.

HOLLYWOOD WITHIN SOCIETY

Hollywood represents the dominance of the ideology of western soci-ety, seen through the eyes of its self-appointed leader. Just as, in the eyes of Americans, the US represents all that is biggest and best in the social culture of the world, so the stars it created acted as symbols of that superiority. They earned the largest salaries, had the most expen-sive clothes, cars and houses. They were designed to be the biggest names in world culture. And in the days before television and wide scale European and Asian film production, American films constituted over 90% of distributed films, with weekly audiences of 500 million.

That the US needed Hollywood to signify what it meant to be 'American' was amply shown by the McCarthy purges in the 1950s, during which Hollywood lost a large number of gifted writers who went back to Europe. (For an account of this, watch the film The Front, 1976, whose writer Walter Bernstein and stars like Zero Mostel were actually blacklisted). On a lesser scale the American nature of Hollywood was seen in all details of the films it produced, and the importance of American cultural leadership was believed and stated by the studios: "Hollywood brings the world to the United States and the United States to the world. This interchange – of writing, brains, talent, music, traditions – is important to world peace. It is equally important to good entertainment which knows no geography and has no international boundary lines." Louis B Mayer (Hollywood October 1937, in McClelland 1986).

The concept of the 'global village' of entertainment has proved to be correct (by the widespread popularity of Walt Disney and Warner Bros cartoons as much as anything else). However, it is naïve to imagine that the US did not have every intention of playing chief landlord to this village as well as bouncer on the village door; responsible for vetting which of the world's 'traditions' were welcome and which were not. This is exactly Richard Dyer's point: "Any dominant ideology in any society presents itself as the ideology of that society as a whole. Its work is to deny the legitimacy of alternate and oppositional ideologies and to construct out of its own contradictions a consensual ideology that will appear to be valid for all members of society." He goes on to underscore the self-contradictory nature of a mass media that tries to sell itself to alternative and subversive ideologies: "As the media must engage with audiences not themselves situated within the dominant groups of society this 'hegemony' is constantly under threat from within and without. Much of the interest of Hollywood lies in this process of contradiction and its 'management." (Dyer, 1998)

The internal contradictions of Hollywood mirrored those of the US as a whole in terms of its handling of ethnic groups, and in this case substantial progress towards restoring the dignity of all members of its population has been made since DW Griffith's 'The Birth of a Nation' and the early 'Cowboys and Indians' movies. The external contradictions have probably made much less progress. Hollywood's recent handling of Tibet, for instance ('Seven Years in Tibet', 1997), is predictably party line. The political contribution of the US to Louis B Mayer's 'world peace' has traditionally been more in trying to unite countries in 'correct' values than in the understanding of the issues that divide world cultures.

Hollywood selects itself for prime sociological consideration by virtue of the amount of product it has created, but the same principles of social psychology apply to other nations. The British, Indian, French and Russian film industries are just as typical of the cultures of those countries, though they would be more reticent about lauding their contributions to 'world peace'. The US might defend its position by saying that since its products, images and the English language itself span the globe it is in a position to offer a 'world culture' with universal values. Other countries might claim that 'universal' was a euphemism for American.

STARS, DISSENT AND THE STATE

At election time in America all the stars come out and party with the politicians, as they do in many other countries. Stars become presidents, mayors and senators. Against this national symbiosis of stars and state, however, the dissenters are also worth mentioning. Rebellion is so much a part of art that it would be surprising not to find the ideological hegemony, as described by Dyer, challenged in some form. The Vietnam war invoked notable protests in America from Jane Fonda and Country Joe and the Fish amongst many others. Often, however, the state was too strong to overcome. Composers Prokofiev and Shostokovich in Russia, and conductor Furtwangler in Hitler's Germany were amongst those who found they had little true freedom from the state in which they had to function. And just as communists left Hollywood, so those wanting a future in the Capitalist world fled in their well-publicised numbers to the West during the time of the Cold War. It is not that art is inherently political in ideology – it is more that the states within which it exists have historically wanted to assert power over it, and in particular the famous people who have acted as its figureheads.

Fame has in this way brought with it a pressure to exist within the parameters of the state. But what if the star in question is better known within the population than its national leader? We remember seeing Michael Jackson on the White House lawn, but do we remember which President was in office at the time? The idea that the private lives of the stars are of more concern than those of the powered elite is stated

Fame

by Alberoni in 'The Powerless Elite' (Alberoni, 1972). It describes stars as a group "whose institutional power is very limited or non-existent, but whose doings and way of life arouse a considerable and sometimes even a maximum degree of interest". Paradoxically, some of the 'powerless elite' have used their fame to actually gain power – Paderewsky, Havel and Reagan became their countries' leaders. Power and stardom, however, (though both may be experienced by the same individual) belong to different social strata. Ignace Paderewsky, having achieved world renown as a concert pianist, found this out when he played for Queen Victoria. As a musician he was placed behind a screen, as befits a mere 'entertainer', so when he was later received by Victoria as Prime Minister of Poland he was unable to resist reminding her pointedly of the incident, saying "no curtain this time, Your Highness?"

STARS AND MINORITY GROUPS

Movie stars have at times had an important role to play as a focus for minority groups – racial, sexual, political and otherwise. Psychological studies on the acceptance of racial groups within society, such as the acceptance of blacks within American society, have shown that one of the crucial factors is the existence of role models at the top levels of that society, (Cook, 1978). When Eddie Murphy became one of the half dozen true stars capable of opening a picture (taking over $20 million in the first week) he finally put black actors right at the top of the star tree. Up until then, the black actor had progressively climbed the star ladder through transitional role models: Paul Robeson (who was politically ostracised for his friendliness with European communist regimes like Russia), Sammy Davis Jr (one of the highest paid entertainers of his generation) Sidney Poitier (who is now an Ambassador for the Bahamas,) and Oprah Winfrey (one of the highest paid TV personalities ever). In sport the domination of blacks within American society has become almost total, needing only Tiger Woods in the sport of golf to become a role model for countless black children and adults alike.

The 'coming out' of movie and sport stars has been equally important for gays and lesbians, though the undeclared homosexuality of famous figures goes considerably further back in history. Transitional figures like Marlene Dietrich and Greta Garbo were adopted as lesbian icons in days long before Anne Heche was a boldly declared lesbian (and suffered more difficulty within the industry for saying so, particularly when playing heterosexual roles). Judy Garland (though heterosexual) was adopted as a gay and cross-dressing icon long before both became commonplace. All paved the way for the open expression of different forms of sexuality in the media or indeed in society as a whole.

Politics has been a more difficult struggle, since more power and control has been exerted by the central authorities, and the power to resist government ideologies has frequently been very limited within the artistic and media communities. The effect of McCarthy on the movie industry in the US was devastating and the waves from this repression continue today. When Elia Kazan – who co-operated with the authorities in identifying suspects – was given a Lifetime Achievement Award at the 1999 Oscars, a number of stars remained seated in protest. Others recognised his own sense of guilt and atonement, as expressed symbolically in 'On the Waterfront'. But there was an industry recognition of the fact that when careers had been ruined and artistic directions irreparably altered, atonement was too little too late. If the public expected their artistic icons to have success in defying the government itself, they were usually bitterly disillusioned.

STARS AND SOCIAL NORMS

Orrin Klapp (Klapp, 1969) suggests three relationships that stars can have with the prevailing social norms:

Reinforcement: Klapp believes that the embodiment of classic social qualities ('the group superself') is the 'natural' role of the hero. Dyer, on the other hand, questions the extent to which the 'hero' would submit to the status quo (Dyer, 1998). A figure such as John Wayne, for instance, conforms politically and ideologically to US 'conservatism', though appears to be independent enough to make up his own mind. Klapp would say he 'happens' to support the status quo, others would question how truly independent his 'independence' was and how truly wide the social and political 'choice' was, from which he chose his particular stance.

Seduction: Klapp divides rebelliousness into the 'seductive' and the 'transcendental', and cites Mickey Spillane and James Bond as examples of the 'seductive' alternative – supporting Oscar Wilde's view that this is the easier option ("The coward does it with a kiss, the brave man with a sword" – 'The Ballad of Reading Gaol'). He states that while "it is possible, permissible, even admirable to romp in the forbidden pasture, the main shortcoming of the seductive hero as teacher is that he leads a person into experience felt traditionally to be wrong but does not redefine or recreate standards by which experience is to be judged. He eludes and confuses morality but makes little contribution to it in terms of insight."

Transcendence: of social norms occurs where the hero "produces a fresh point of view, a feeling of integrity, and makes a new man", a process without the charm or sidestepping of seduction in which alternative norms are inescapably obvious, and carry their social consequences. (Klapp, 1969, pp227–9).

These categories are more thought provoking than exhaustive. How would they, for instance, explain the reaction to OJ Simpson's arrest and trial in the black community? There was a quality of seduction in the movie like car chase and the fact that Simpson had been known for comedy roles in the 'Naked Gun' movies. There was an implied idea that he 'transcended' the LAPD, which was considered by blacks to be notoriously racially biased, as evidenced by contemporaneous video footage of black suspect Rodney King being beaten up by police. But there was no transcendence of social norms in the sense of providing deeper insight or better alternatives.

Transcendence is clearly essential in the creative hall of fame. Major artistic and social landmarks like Stravinsky's 'Rite of Spring', Freud's 'Psychopathology of Everyday Life', or Charles Darwin's 'Origin of Species', not only met with considerable public commotion and disbelief, they established viable new ways of looking at our human world which have stood the test of time. Whether it can be done to anything like the same extent in the movie world is doubtful. For a start, the committee nature of movie making – from the splitting of the script itself between several different writers to the constant creative arguments at direction and production level – would make a single coherent viewpoint difficult. And even then the entertainment needs of the movie and the need to recoup financial investment would severely mitigate against a 'new' and coherent social view and indeed the profundity necessary to back it up with true insight.

Some films have been considered social milestones in the cinema ('Cathy Come Home', 'The Grapes of Wrath', 'Modern Times',

'Metropolis'), but their actual impact has been relatively slight, and their heroes are in the final analysis simply actors portraying a point of view. Exceptions to this may be films like DW Griffith's 'The Birth of a Nation', which is credited by some sociologists of the cinema with the resurgence of the Ku Klux Klan, and 'Triumph of the Will' which is credited with inciting anti-Semitism. But even then it could be argued that these social changes were already in motion and that the films simply echoed them. If we take a wider brief, we might see 'capitalist cinema' as a social force in poor countries, a view Sukarno shared: "The motion picture industry has provided a window on the world, and the colonised nations have looked through that window and have seen the things of which they have been deprived. It is perhaps not generally realised that a refrigerator can be a revolutionary symbol to a people who have no refrigerators. Hollywood helped to build up the sense of deprivation of man's birthright, and that sense of deprivation has played a large part in the national revolutions of postwar Asia." (McLuhan and Fiore, 1967)

Where actors themselves have been truly brave they have often been ostracised, as in the case of Paul Robeson, or greeted with a mixture of respect and reservation, such as Brando for his stance on Native Americans or Jane Fonda for her anti-war views. Their relationship with the public may include what Dyer calls "compensation" (Dyer, 1998, pp 28–9). They stand for values that the public itself would like to express but cannot or lack the courage to express, such as anti-government views or defence of social minorities. In the case of the youthful Brando it was an irreverent social 'attitude', as when in his early days he would turn up unshaven at parties and behave much as he wanted. Such compensation may be particularly true of the relationship between teenagers and their idols, in which the teenage need for 'irreverent' role models may largely be met by quite superficial aspects of stars and celebrities like tattoos, body piercings, foul language and wacky or grungy clothes. Their real need for alternative and coherent social values would not in general be understood at that stage of maturity however much it may be sensed as morally right, as when thousands of teenagers marched against the Bomb in the 1960s. Sometimes, as with the young Bob Dylan, Joan Baez and John Lennon, both star and public were involved in a continual social experiment whose full ideology took years of change and development to mature.

Fame

STARS AS SYMBOLS OF SUCCESS

On another level, the star symbolises the Western myth of success, and reassures the public that there is a real chance that given luck or 'breaks' (chance encounters with stars, agents and talent scouts) and of course hard work, success is quite possible. The inherent contradiction lies first in whether the star, who comes out of the 'people', is especially talented. But beyond that is a further contradiction, as expressed by psychologist Julian Rotter in his 'Locus of Control Scale' (Rotter, 1966), which lies between the opposite poles of Internal (I shape my own destiny) and External (my destiny is shaped by fate and external variables).

The success myth is built on the 'Internal' western culture of self control, epitomised by hard work and equal opportunity and reinforced by concepts such as being able to buy what you want and insuring against loss. But 'lucky breaks' are 'External', and much nearer the Eastern or Zen spiritual cultures. Success may in fact depend on an interrelation between Internal and External control, expressed by phrases like 'It's funny – the more I practise, the luckier I get' (attributed to various sportspeople) and "Chance favours only the prepared mind." (Louis Pasteur, Address to the University of Lille, 1854). 'Genetic advantage', a further dimension, is Internal in that it is in every gene, though it is not yet under the control of humans. Karma is another wholly different concept, with a spiritual dimension of its own.

The general public, however, seems just as at home with this paradoxical concept of success as both reachable and unreachable as they do with the National Lottery, in which the chances of winning are five times less than being struck by lightning. The same public has an insatiable interest in the Rich and Famous (the R+F), reads the social whirl of Hello! magazine with gusto, buys magazines featuring stately homes and their owners week in week out and idolises star icons like Elizabeth Taylor who is more married, more divorced, more beautiful, more well connected, and more ostentatiously expensive than they will ever be. One way in which the public may reconcile this within themselves is by believing that money and success does not really alter the star – deep down they remain just as ordinary as the rest of us, and so any of us could 'be' that star. Sometimes this is expressed as a transitory phenomenon – Warhol's 'famous for 15 minutes' or the transposition of the Prince and the Pauper, or Cinderella and the Princess, in which we can morph temporarily between one state and another.

In another sense the public sees the whole entertainment business as a form of seduction, in which people - however rich they are - never have 'a proper job', contribute little to society and are merely 'posturing' opinions. As one experienced rock musician put it: "Most people regard musicians as one step up the social ladder from rapists and muggers, and it's this alienation from the non-musician that I believe creates most of the problems. The public judge a musician only by the money he earns. If he's rich, he's a great man. If he's poor, he's a time-wasting parasite who should get a 'real' job. Even despite the purely economic fact that Elton John has probably paid more tax than Wigan and brought in more foreign earnings than British Steel, it is not a 'real' job!" (Wills and Cooper, 1988) In other words none of it is serious, and it all exists outside present day realities.

STARS AS 'SOCIAL TYPES'

One explanation of stars, as fitting the 'star as a phenomenon of consumption', is the idea that they are necessary because they represent certain social types. Social history reveals several successive systems of social typing. Even leaving out phrenology, we have early systems like the humours – Bilious, Sanguine, Phlegmatic and Choleric. We then have Earth, Water, Fire and Air, which are further differentiated by the twelve astrological signs, which contain three of each. There are the Tao types. And there are the psychological types – the 16 types of the Myers Briggs Type Indicator and the Parent, Adult and Child Ego States of Transactional Analysis (James and Jongeward, 1978) which may predominate in the characters of people. Historically we have pursued this process of categorisation, though the typology varies. People are assigned to their types in different ways – by word of mouth with the humours, by birth time with the Astrological signs, by psychometric questionnaire with the Myers Briggs, by analysis of the 'transactions' they make with Transactional Analysis.

There is a small amount of mileage in the idea that we self-identify with our 'type', inasmuch as we can actually determine our type. This can be done with astrology because birth dates of stars are known, and there is a corresponding amount of literature on this theme. Theoretically, it could be done with the Myers Briggs typology. However, few MBTI 'types' of stars are known and this system – though strongly defended by its fans – enjoys nowhere near the popularity of astrology, partly because the mechanics of determining 'type' are, like most psychometric materials, not freely available to the general public.

In the absence of verifiable types (such as the Myers Briggs), media studies literature has presented 'anecdotal' types, such as the Hero, the Villain and the Fool (Klapp, 1962). More 'cinematic' categories include the Good Joe (John Wayne, Bob Hope), the Tough Guy (James Cagney, Clint Eastwood), the Pinup (Marilyn Monroe, Jane Fonda) the Rebel (Marlon Brando, James Dean) and the Independent Woman (Bette Davis, Katherine Hepburn). This system is manifestly far from perfect in that there are so many overlaps (Eastwood as the Rebel, Fonda as the Independent Woman, Wayne as the Tough Guy).

If there is any truth in the whole concept of typology it lies more in the dynamic identification of type than the static 'personality' one. We identify more with how our heroes act. Wayne is the Good Joe when he upholds traditional values, but the Rebel when he challenges. Fonda is the Pinup when she is expressing her natural sexuality but Independent when she marches against social issues. This is much closer to the Transactional Analysis system in which Monroe and the sexual Fonda would be the Natural Child, Eastwood the Rebellious Child and Good Joe the Adapted Child. Wayne as the strong and wise problem solver would then be the Adult, while the Critical Parent would be Mrs Danvers in 'Rebecca' and the Nurturing Parent would be someone with heart and soul like Shelley Winters. The TA model has added sophistication in the form of 'scripts' which are founded on historic myths like Hercules or Sisyphus and go some way towards defining many movie plots ('Rambo', 'On the Waterfront').

In the final analysis such generalisations about social types and how they react dynamically to the situations they get into, while endlessly interesting, have to be considered alongside the psychological theories which centre on the unique charisma of the stars themselves and which fill volume after volume of star biographies.

REFERENCES

Alberoni, F (1972) *The Powerless Elite*, in McQuail D (ed.) Sociology of Mass Communications, London, Penguin

Aument, J-P (1997) *Suns and Shadows*

Bartlett, D, Kaufman, D, and Smeltekop, R (1993) *The effects of music listening and perceived sensory experiences on the immune system as measured by interleukin and cortisol.* Journal of Music Therapy 30, 194-209

Berne, Eric (1964) *Games People Play*, Harmondwsorth, Penguin

Boller and Davis (1987) *Hollywood Anecdotes* London: Macmillan.

Cary, Diana Serra (1978) Hollywood's Children - *An Inside Account of the Child Star Era* Dallas, Southern Methodist University Press

Cook, SW (1978) *Interpersonal and attitudinal outcomes in co-operating interracial groups.* Journal of Research and Development in Education, 12 pp 97-113

Dyer, Richard (1998) *Stars*, London, British Film Institute Publishing

Etcoff, N (1999) *Survival of the Fittest: The Science of Beauty*

Evans, Andrew (1994) *The Secrets of Musical Confidence*, London, HarperCollins

James, Muriel and Jongeward, Dorothy (1978) *Born to Win*, London, Signet

Kent, Nicolas (1991) *Naked Hollywood*, London, BBC Books

Klapp, Orrin (1969) *Collective Search for Identity*, NY, Holt, Rinehart and Winston

Klapp, Orrin (1962) *Heroes, Villains and Fools*, Englewood Cliffs, NJ, Prentice-Hall

McLuhan, M and Fiore, Q(1967) *The Medium is the Massage*, London, Penguin Books

McClelland, Doug (1985) *Hollywood on Hollywood - Tinsel Town Talks* Winchester MA USA:
Faber and Faber

Monroe, Marilyn (1983) *In her own words*

Myers, IB and PB(1980) *Gifts Differing*, Palo Alto, Consulting Psychologists Press

Powdermaker, Hortense (1950) *The Dream Factory*, Boston, Little Brown

Rotter, JB (1966) *Generalised expectancies for internal versus external control of reinforcement.* Psychological Monographs 80

Fame

Shuter-Dyson, R and Gabriel, C (1981) *The Psychology of Musical Ability* (2nd edition), London, Methuen

Todd, Anne (1980) *The Eighth Veil*

Wills, Geoff and Cooper, Cary (1988) *Pressure Sensitive*, London, Sage Books

THE DOWNSIDE OF FAME

To the public at large it seems that being famous is an ideal state. And, indeed, when people who are not born into public life are first rocketed to stardom they usually experience a great high. But it so often happens that this does not last as they have difficulty coping with their new-found fame and various negative aspects of the condition begin to catch up with them.

In some respects the experience of lottery and pools winners is prototypic. At first they are 'over the moon' with delight, but being unused to handling wealth, many of them make errors in adjusting their lifestyle that result in them being less happy than they were before they won. One error is to squander the money. Reckless spending can quickly deplete what initially seemed to be a fortune. Another error is to cut contact with old friends, family and the familiar neighbourhood in order to relocate among rich people in a fantasy paradise such as Florida. It often happens that the new neighbours are not friendly to these 'nouveau riche' and subsequently they have difficulty with social integration. They then find that the climatic advantages do not offset the need for social support, but it is too late because they have burned their bridges (possibly having insulted friends and work mates in their local community). Other lottery winners report that they can no longer feel comfortable with people because they cannot distinguish their true friends from those who are after a handout. Put these various effects together and many of them are left ruing the day they came into money. A group of New York Lotto winners actually formed a self-help group in order to deal with what they called 'post-lottery depression syndrome'.

Much the same applies to many pop singers and sports stars who have come from humble backgrounds and are unable to cope with sudden fame. Deprived of realistic feedback from those around them, they experience disorientation and identity problems. Some become arrogant, rude and anti-social, believing that their fame entitles them to behave badly – attacking photographers, breaking up furniture in restaurants, discarding agents and managers who have helped to make them successful, and so on. Others turn to drink and drugs or become depressed and suicidal.

BIG HEADS BUT FRAGILE EGOS?

One of the hazards of becoming famous may be a slide towards self-absorption. Anecdotes of the narcissism and grandiosity of the stars are abundant. Reviewing the autobiography of Kenneth Williams ('Just Williams', 1985) in The Sunday Times, George Melly noted that although "living through almost 60 years of turbulent history and profound social change, he [Williams] recorded no thoughts on anything unrelated to himself". In his 'Diaries' (1993) the world's worst plane crash – in which 574 people were burnt to death in Tenerife a few minutes after he landed there – is mentioned only as the reason his bags were delayed, causing him to be furious about having to go to bed without washing or changing properly. John F. Kennedy was reportedly so fond of his own image that he had the White House filled with mirrors so that he could admire himself frequently. Marilyn Monroe regarded herself as so indispensable that she would almost invariably arrive late on a film set, or not at all, if she felt disinclined. According to Norman Mailer, during the filming of 'Some Like It Hot', "on a good day she was two hours late, on a bad day, six." Val Kilmer is said to have had film crews and extras at Pinewood Studios instructed not to make eye contact with him. This may have been one of the traits prompting Marlon Brando to remark that Kilmer was "confusing the size of his talent with the size of his pay cheque" (The Sunday Times, 25/8/96). Elton John tells the story himself that once when he was staying at the Inn on the Park in London it was very windy outside, so he phoned down to the desk and asked them to stop the wind (The Observer, 5/3/95). In all these cases, the observation that these celebrities 'have become too big for their boots' needs to be tempered with a recognition of their underlying vulnerability.

Although there appears to be a connection between stardom and self-centredness, it is not always clear which is the cause and which the effect. People with high estimates of their self-worth, and who use other people cynically, may increase their chances of achieving fame. "Success didn't spoil me; I've always been insufferable," joked Fran Lebowitz. But it is equally true that many people who acquire celebrity status grow progressively self-indulgent and arrogant. In fact, there are clear parallels between the characteristics of individuals suffering from narcissistic personality disorder and those of certain famous people who are obsessed with publicity and power. Both are manipulative in milking others for attention and vindictive to those thought to have unjustly obstructed or humiliated them, or even to have withheld proper adulation. Both appear superficially boastful and big-headed, yet are likely to harbour fundamental insecurity. Both exhibit outlandish and self-destructive behaviour in an increasingly desperate bid to wrench attention from a neglectful public. Both seem to need the reactions of others to affirm their own existence. 'People are noticing me – therefore I am!'

Even if a performer does not start out being narcissistic, some progression of this kind may be almost inevitable. An environment such as Hollywood is highly competitive, so people are bound to pursue various forms of self-improvement: diets, body-building, cosmetic surgery, psychotherapy, and so forth. In order to survive, it is essential to be one of 'the beautiful people'. As social contacts are so critical, the tendency to move among influential people who may help one's career can result in an inability to sustain real, meaningful, social relationships. Performing also breeds self-consciousness in that a requirement of the art is to see oneself as others see one. This is tantamount to holding an imaginary mirror in front of oneself. The self-consciousness that is elevated by these experiences may not be identical to narcissism but can certainly contribute to it.

Thus, it seems that the rise to fame may often be accompanied by an unhealthy obsession with the self, intensified and encouraged in the Hollywood environment, and also an insensitivity to the feelings of others coupled by an arrogance that is off-putting to others. Along with addiction to success and manipulative strategies for achieving it, these traits can result in a loss of true friends and the important emotional support that they provide. Ultimately, this may cause isolation and despair. As PG Wodehouse once said, "The usual drawback to success is that it annoys one's friends so". Despite all the attention of media and public, life at the top can be quite lonely.

THE PUBLIC EYE

According to comedian Fred Allen, a celebrity is "a person who strives to become well known, then wears dark glasses in order to avoid being recognised". There is more than an element of truth in this. Having achieved great fame with the help of the media, many stars then resent the constant intrusion on their private lives. They feel pressured by the constant gaze of the public, beleaguered by their fans and that, generally, their lives are no longer their own. As singer Tiny Tim put it,

Fame

"celebrities cannot have private lives. They have to give that up. When I have a spat with my wife, the press will know it. If I'm not good in bed – which I'm not – the press will know it" (Hurley, 1988). Perhaps the ultimate in voyeuristic invasion of privacy occurred when President Clinton was asked detailed questions, under oath and on nationwide TV, about his inventive ways of using cigars in the Oval Office.

Celebrities react in various ways to this feeling of intrusion. Some, like Greta Garbo, Lon Chaney, Elvis Presley, Doris Day and Howard Hughes become reclusive. This strategy may be counterproductive, as in the cases of film producer Stanley Kubrick and novelist JD Salinger, who became even more famous as recluses. Other stars react with aggression, insulting autograph hunters, punching photographers, or suing the magazines that write about them. The public has usually taken the attitude that they have a right to follow the movements of stars; that they have renounced their claim to privacy and effectively become 'public property'. At other times, most notably in the wake of the car crash that killed Diana, Princess of Wales, the relentless pursuit of the paparazzi has been roundly condemned.

There are cultural variations in the behaviour of the media. The exploits of entertainers have always been fair game. After all, a degree of moral degeneracy is reckoned as par for their course. With respect to politicians, the French press has generally been discreet and continues to be today. The womanising of prominent figures such as Lloyd George in Britain and JF Kennedy in the US was also left in the private domain. Watersheds seemed to occur with the Profumo affair in Britain and Gary Hart in the US, after which politicians and royalty have been subjected to the closest scrutiny. Clinton seemed to be a victim of the convergence of political correctness with increasing media surveillance, while Princess Diana had come to occupy the role of Marilyn Monroe as the perennially unloved and vulnerable woman. Today there are intense debates about how to strike an appropriate balance between press freedom and individual privacy. Some have suggested extending anti-stalking laws to reporters and photographers and the banning of listening devices and long-range lenses. Others have defended their 'right to know' about the behaviour of those in privileged positions, arguing that the public interest cannot be distinguished from the interest of the public.

The Downside of Fame

The famous are understandably concerned about the impact their own publicity may have upon their children. Many people will recall the tragic case of Charles Lindbergh, the aviation pioneer. Lindbergh was a shy man who hated the limelight. He remained taciturn through his hero's welcome in the US after his solo cross-Atlantic flight in 1927, to the annoyance of the press, and sought privacy in Japan. Unfortunately, this did not prevent the kidnapping and murder of his baby in 1932. Not surprisingly, the children of celebrities (eg Chelsea Clinton and Princes William and Harry) need special protection. At the very least, they are embarrassed by the seemingly inevitable revelations concerning the complicated sex lives of their parents.

There is little doubt that the feeling of 'living in a goldfish bowl' is a major source of stress to many stars. To some, who deliberately sought stardom, it is usually an unanticipated side-effect. To others, such as John McCarthy (held hostage by Muslim extremists in Lebanon) and possibly Monica Lewinsky (Clinton's 'intern'), having fame thrust upon them may be even more unwelcome because exhibitionism is not necessarily part of their nature. Lewinsky was reduced to tears by the questions thrown at her by the media during her first British book signing session at Harrods.

Press intrusion is particularly problematic for celebrities who are concerned with concealing some aspect of their sexuality, for example affairs, promiscuity, homosexual cruising. In 1995 Hugh Grant's acting career and relationship with model Liz Hurley were jeopardised when he was caught with a prostitute, Divine Brown, in a car in Hollywood. She, of course, became famous. In the days of Montgomery Clift, Rock Hudson and Liberace, not to mention Rudolph Valentino, it was almost essential to hide homosexuality, and great energy was expended in doing so. Many stars were forced into sham marriages by their studios in an attempt of cover a gay orientation.

And even today, stars have more or less traumatic 'outings'. Michael Barrymore lost his marriage and almost his career as a comedian after the unpremeditated exposure of his homosexual preference during a performance at a gay pub in London's East End. The singer George Michael only conceded he was gay after a humiliating arrest for 'lewd behaviour' in a Los Angeles public toilet. When the former Welsh Secretary, Ron Davies, had his car stolen in South London, his attempts to conceal the fact that he had been cruising on Clapham

Fame

Common at the time triggered his resignation from the Labour Government.

FRIGHT AND FLIGHT

A particular kind of public scrutiny that distresses many performers is that of their audience and critics. Stage fright affects many great performers, even at the top of their career. Lord Olivier, Richard Burton, David Niven and Sergei Rachmaninov are among the big names that have fallen foul of this affliction. It may be constant from their earliest days, escalate slowly and progressively, or appear suddenly from nowhere. Around one-third of actors, singers and dancers suffer some degree of performance anxiety, and about half of all instrumental musicians (Marchant-Haycox and Wilson, 1992). One American study found that 27% of musicians were taking beta-blockers under prescription, despite the fact that they are known to trigger asthmatic attacks and that the US Federal Drugs Administration does not approve the use of these drugs for stage fright (Fishbein, et al ,1988).

Stage fright takes many forms. For Olivier it seemed to be centred around the fear of forgetting his lines. "My cue came, and I went onto that stage where I knew with grim certainty I would not be capable of remaining more than a few minutes. I began to watch for the instant at which my knowledge of the next line would vanish.... My voice started to fade, my throat closed up and the audience was beginning to go giddily round." (Olivier, 1982) More commonly it focuses on heightened awareness of the audience and a fear of negative evaluation. "Why had I ever become an actress? I would die, drowned by the laughter of three thousand people who would discover my incompetence at first glance... Somehow I managed the fifty steps to the centre of the stage. Fainting seemed to be the only escape." (Heinze, 1994)

In both of these instances the performer was able to carry on, but for others the anticipated catastrophe does occur. In 1967, during a concert at New York's Central Park, with 135,000 people in the audience, Barbra Streisand forgot the words to one of her songs. The shock was such that she refused to sing another live concert for 27 years. Daniel Day-Lewis walked out in the middle of a performance of 'Hamlet' at the National Theatre in 1989 believing that he had seen the ghost of his own dead father, the poet Cecil Day-Lewis. Ian Holm froze in mid-monologue during a performance of 'The Iceman Cometh', an experience that kept him off the stage for 15 years. Nicol Williamson, Jonathan Pryce and John Sessions are among many others to have lost their cool on occasion to the extent of walking off the stage. Other well-known performers, including John Lennon, Cher and Sex Pistol John Lydon, were said to suffer severe gastro-intestinal disturbances before performances, causing vomiting or diarrhoea.

Some top performers experience a resistance to public appearance that psychologists call "reactive inhibition" (a particular form of burn-out). This is characterised by a feeling of having reached a plateau at the top of one's career, where there is no further reward to be gained by carrying on repeating the same old skills. It may be compounded by a feeling that the media, which helped put one on the pedestal, are now conspiring to knock one off it again. This is likely to be true for people who are so good, and have reached such dizzy heights of fame, that only a disaster is newsworthy. Sports stars are particularly prone to this form of burn-out because great effort is needed to keep themselves in peak condition and to motivate themselves for each new competition. England cricketer Len Hutton once had to be pulled out of bed to play in a test match against Australia, apparently because he was frightened of batting and Bjorn Borg retired prematurely from competitive tennis claiming exhaustion. Superstars perhaps detect that the media and the fans can be fickle; David Beckham and Will Carling were two who experienced a most spectacular fall from grace after what might be regarded as relatively minor misdemeanours.

A rather dramatic reaction to professional pressure is actual flight from the stressful environment. A famous instance is that of Agatha Christie, who disappeared from her Surrey home in the 1920s, apparently unable to cope with the combination of her new-found fame as a best-selling crime writer and her marriage problems. A police search was launched and she was not found until 10 days later when she was located staying at a Harrogate hotel after a tip-off from a waitress who recognised her photo in the newspaper. More recently, actress Julia Roberts fled from a film set and hid in Ireland after the break-up of her engagement to Kiefer Sutherland. When comedian Stephen Fry received poor reviews for his performance in the play 'Cell Mates' he absconded to Europe leaving fellow performers in the lurch and his friends fearing suicide. None of these escapes corresponded to the clinical condition known as "fugue", in that there was no claim of amnesia for the previous life. They do, however, seem more common in actors because an element of dissociation seems to be involved and they are properly considered stress-induced breakdowns rather than simple petulance.

The term "lost bottle panic" may be applied to various reactions linked to stage fright, burn-out, and fears for the future. This may be precipitated by unrealistic career demands, having to learn roles and musical scores by heart, preparing numerous speeches, busy travel and engagement schedules stretching years into the future, and constant expectations of excellence. Fears are compounded by recognition of the cruel ravages of the ageing process. There is the physical loss of function (especially critical for dancers and sports stars), deterioration of memory, declining passion and energy, and recognition of the fact that the public and producers alike constantly seek youth. Some accept the transition to middle age gracefully; others (like the fictional Norma Desmond in 'Sunset Boulevard') retreat into a world of delusion. The loss of youthful beauty seemed to cause Brigitte Bardot to retreat into the company of animals and promotion of animal rights. The desire to escape by one means or another is perfectly understandable.

WHO AM I?
An interesting aspect of the disappearance of Stephen Fry is that it echoed the flight of the character he was playing, the spy George Blake. Before the play opened Fry had noted in interviews certain similarities between himself and Blake, claiming "we are both outsiders, being Jewish and a woofter". To this one might add that they were both in the business of fantasy or deception (Fry admitted that as an actor he often felt like a fake). Blake fled to Russia after his espionage was unmasked, and it is easy to suppose that Fry's disappearance might have been in some sense primed by the role he was playing.

There are more striking examples than this. In Brazil a young soap actor apparently killed his on-screen girl friend after she ended their fictional relationship. After filming the episode in which he was rejected, Guilherme de Padua burst into tears and refused to speak to anyone. Later that day the body of his co-star Daniella Perez was found on wasteland near the studios having been stabbed 18 times with scissors. Witnesses told police they had seen Padua wait for her, hit her and bundle her into his car. Padua initially confessed to acting alone, then later tried to implicate his estranged wife (The Sunday Times, 25/8/96). To all appearances this was a tragic instance of an actor over-identifying with the role he was playing.

It is not unusual for the viewing public to confuse fiction with reality, especially as dramas become more realistic and documentaries are increasingly exposed as having been faked in some degree. Most soap actors can tell of instances where people have reacted to them as if they were responsible for things their character has done; those who play villainous roles get many threats. This can significantly add to the problems performers sometimes have in disentangling themselves from their screen persona. Several actors and actresses have felt 'possessed' by the part they were playing and unable to extricate themselves from it. For example, Mel Martin who portrayed Vivien Leigh in a TV biography called 'Darling of the Gods' (1990) told The Sun newspaper that she talked to Vivien and heard her voice telling her how to act in different scenes. "I did not play Vivien Leigh, I became her. There were spells when her spirit took me over and I'm not sure I'll ever be totally free of her." This condition has also been observed in undercover cops who have been required to immerse themselves convincingly in criminal subcultures for long periods of time. When the time comes for them to return to their previous, respectable lives they are liable to experience "re-entry strain", which is sometimes sufficient to trigger schizophrenia. (Girodo, 1984)

Loy and Brown (1982) analysed the fate of female musical comedy stars around the turn of the century. They found that women like Sophie Tucker, Anna Held and Julia Sanderson were initially attracted to the personal independence and public glamour offered by life on the stage. However, this independent status led to them being labelled as deviants within a male-dominated society and they became stereotyped as figures of male fantasy. Each became caught up in this role to the extent that it took over their offstage lives, controlled their sexual and social relationships, and ultimately denied them the autonomy and self-expression they had sought. It is a great paradox that many people seek fame and wealth in order to gain freedom from the demands of others, only to discover a new set of pressures and constraints.

Those who get type cast, playing much the same role over and over, are particularly likely to lose sight of their true self. After all, the role they are called upon to perform is not necessarily similar to their real personality. Those who play a variety of different roles may also lose touch of who they really are. Peter Sellers once said he never knew who he was until he put on a moustache, a hat, an accent or a silly walk; his discomfort at trying to be himself on chat shows was clear to see. Celebrities are confused and irritated by the fact that everybody knows who they are and behaves as though they expect reciprocation. And, as already noted, people who suddenly become rich and famous often experience such a detachment from their previous selves that they are left confused and frightened. These various identification problems can greatly increase the stress experienced by stars.

THE DRUG CULTURE

A response to stress and mode of detachment from reality that becomes a major problem in its own right for many stars is drug dependency. Drugs (as with alcohol) are easily affordable for wealthy celebrities and readily available at the sort of parties and social events they attend. The habit often starts out as recreational but addiction takes over. The stress of late night appearances, audience expectations, busy schedules and the need to hype oneself up when feeling low may all contribute to the high rate of addiction among performers. Judy Garland and Marilyn Monroe are famous instances of major stars who appeared to get onto a treadmill of substance abuse which they believed was essential to their survival, but which ended tragically.

The pop music and jazz scenes are particularly notorious for drug abuse (Wills and Cooper, 1988). Noel Gallagher of Oasis is quoted as saying that for him taking drugs is no different from "having a cup of tea". Even members of the audience at pop concerts often take drugs and there is a widespread belief that drugs such as ecstasy, LSD and cocaine can provide inspiration for performers by expanding consciousness and increasing extraversion. This is possibly true in the early stages of creativity, for drugs, like mild degrees of psychoticism, can be a source of originality (Brian Wilson of The Beach Boys and possibly also The Beatles) but they are almost certain to be destructive in the long run.

The list of pop stars who have notoriously been involved with drugs is considerable. Jimi Hendrix used drugs of all kinds to energise his guitar playing before choking on his own vomit at the age of 27. Kurt

Cobain, leader of the American 'grunge' trio Nirvana, was also just 27 and addicted to heroin and barbiturates when he blew off his head with a shotgun. Others who have died young in the thrall of drugs are Brian Jones, Keith Moon, Jim Morrison, Janis Joplin, Al Wilson, Paul Kossoff and Michael Hutchence. Elvis Presley might also be included in this group, though the role of drugs in the failure of his health remains mysterious (an addiction to fast foods such as hamburgers may have been a factor). Eric Clapton and Elton John are among many pop stars who have admitted problems with drugs and alcohol but survived to counsel against them.

Many actors have also experienced problems with drugs. John Belushi, the comedian who starred in 'The Blues Brothers', died in 1982 from massive overdoses of amphetamine, cocaine and heroin. River Phoenix collapsed and died on a Hollywood pavement from a fatal cocktail of drugs at the tender age of 23, and Australian soap star Jason Donovan was carried from a nightclub on a stretcher in 1995 and rushed to hospital after a cocaine binge. Great actors who were almost as famous for their drinking as their talent include Montgomery Clift, Richard Burton, Robert Shaw, Richard Harris, Peter O'Toole, Oliver Reed, Robert Stephens and Brian Cox. (Most of these managed to control their habit sufficiently to continue their careers and some made brilliant recoveries). The Betty Ford Clinic, specialising in the treatment of alcoholism and drug addiction, boasts many celebrities among its clients, including Peter Lawford, Elizabeth Taylor and Liza Minelli (daughter of Judy Garland). Of course, the booze and drug adventures of the famous gain more press coverage than those of the unemployed, but among the professional classes performers, and especially those at the top, seem highly susceptible.

DOWN AND OFTEN OUT

One of the reasons often suggested for substance abuse among the famous, apart from stress and temptation, is depression. Indeed, addiction sometimes seems to represent a slow, virtual suicide. It might seem extraordinary to the rest of us that stars and celebrities, who on the face of it, have everything going for them (fame, wealth, looks), should so often appear to be utterly miserable. Yet there is some evidence that this is so, and presumably for the reasons outlined above. It is a truism that money cannot buy happiness.

Fame

Margot Kidder, who played Superman's girlfriend Lois Lane, could not work and went bankrupt as a result of severe manic-depression and paranoia. Convinced that her husband was trying to kill her, she wandered the streets living as one of the homeless. In 1996 she was found by police in a distressed state, having cut her hair off with a razor blade, and hiding under a porch near the studio where 'Superman' had been filmed. She claimed to have been stalked and attacked but there was little evidence to back this up. Placed in psychiatric care she was able to make a good recovery and get her career back on track. Others who were hospitalised, or suffered from serious depression at certain times in their lives, include Audie Murphy, Gene Tierney, Audrey Hepburn, Vivien Leigh, and Spike Milligan.

Comedians may be particularly susceptible to depression. They often complain that people expect them to be funny at all times, even when they are feeling miserable. The stereotype of the unhappy clown is well known and is supported in a study by Janus (1975). He found that 85% of a sample of male comedians had sought psychotherapy at some time in their lives. It may be the case that jokers have developed humour as a buffer against fundamental unhappiness or because their jokes often make play of, and therefore continuously rub in, their own deficiencies: Oliver Hardy's fatness, Woody Allen's insecurity about his sexual prowess, Jack Benny's meanness and inadequacy as a violinist, Rodney Dangerfield's failure to garner respect, John Cleese's crippling concern for respectability, the gender ambiguity of Kenneth Williams and Frankie Howard, and so on. The emphasis on these traits, which often originate in reality, may ultimately cause self-esteem to collapse. Tony Hancock's lonely suicide in an Australian hotel bedroom seems to typify the frequent failure of a comedian's defences to save himself from the perception of utter gloom.

Suicide rates are high among celebrities in general. Besides Marilyn Monroe and those who were cited in connection with drug abuse, and comedians Tony Hancock and Kenneth Williams, there was Carole Landis, Gig Young, George Sanders, Charles Boyer, George Reeves (the first Superman, whom some say was murdered), Pier Angeli (some say because she was afraid of reaching 40), Margaux Hemingway (who had a family history of suicide), Capucine, Romy Schneider, Abbie Hoffman, Mary Millington, Rachel Roberts, Bobbie Driscoll, Del Shannon, Lennie Bruce, Vincent Van Gogh, Freddie Mills (boxer), Sylvia Plath (poet),

David Rappaport (diminutive actor), Pete Duel and Brian Keith. This of course is only a partial list. A study at the University of Houston by Professor Jib Fowles found that the stars who died between 1964 and 1983 were four times as likely to have killed themselves than the average American (Hurley, 1988).

In some instances the suicide seems to have occurred in response to career paralysis (Anger, 1975). Alan Ladd, at one time the highest paid star in Hollywood, who was a heavy drinker and insecure about his height (5' 4"), appears to have killed himself after his appearance with George Peppard in 'The Carpetbaggers' failed to deliver the hoped for revival of his career. Peg Entwistle, a failed starlet from England, would certainly never have been remembered but for the manner of her suicide – jumping off the top of the 50ft high HOLLYWOOD sign in 1932, after a night of drinking and feeling depressed. Then there was Lupe Velez, a beautiful, sexy Mexican star of silent movies who couldn't succeed with the advent of the talkies. Intent on a glamorous departure, she bedecked herself in a stunning silver lame nightdress and had her hair and make-up professionally done, before taking an overdose of sleeping pills. Unfortunately, the drugs reacted badly with the last (Mexican) meal she had eaten, and she was found in a most undignified posture, head first in the toilet bowl.

These last two examples hint that suicide among top performers may be a final exhibitionistic gesture, consistent with the histrionic personalities that inhabit the theatre and film world. This might help to explain the apparent high rates of early death and suicide among celebrities. Perhaps there is something in the nature of some famous people that makes them want to be noticed even for the manner of their death. Cleopatra was greatly concerned about dignity in death. Rather than suffer the humiliation of being paraded through Rome by Octavius after military defeat at Actium, she committed suicide by snake bite, having first dressed in her royal finery and ensured that her hand-maiden would lay her out decorously. Perhaps some starlets prefer death to being paraded in defeat by Chronos?

It would be possible to list many other celebrities who have experienced difficulty or come to some kind of a sticky end, but enough has been said to illustrate the fact that life at the top is not necessarily a bed of flowers. At least the roses have thorns. As already noted, the disasters that befall the superstars gain more media attention than the

Fame

afflictions of ordinary people, so it is easy to get them out of propor-tion. It is also possible that we have selective interest in the troubles of celebrities just to reassure ourselves that our lot in life is not all that inferior. Despite all, though, it does seem that the famous have more than their share of travails, and a great many are, like those who defile the tombs of the Pharaohs, fatally cursed.

REFERENCES

Anger, K (1975) *Hollywood Babylon San Francisco*: Straight Arrow Books.

Davies, R (ed.) (1993) *The Kenneth Williams Diaries*. London: Harper Collins.

Fishbein, M, Middlestadt SE, Otatti V, Strauss S, and Ellis A (1988) *Medical problems among ICSOM musicians: overview of a national survey*. Medical Problems of Performing Artists, 3, 1–8.

Girodo, M (1984) Entry and re-entry strain in undercover agents. In Allen, VL and Van der Vliert, E (eds.) *Role Transitions*. New York: Plenum.

Heinze, RI (1994) *The Light in the Dark: The Search for Visions*. Berkeley: Independent Scholars of Asia.

Hurley, D (1988) *The end of celebrity*. Psychology Today, 22, 50–55.

Janus, SS (1975) *The great comedians: personality and other factors*. American Journal of Psychoanalysis, 35, 169–174.

Loy, P and Brown, J (1982) *Red hot mamas, sex kittens and sweet young things: Role engulfment in the lives of musical comedy performers*. International Journal of Women's Studies. 5, 338–347.

Marchant-Haycoxb SE and Wilson G.D. (1992) *Personality and stress in performing artists. Personality and Individual Differences*. 13, 1061–1068.

Olivier, L (1982) *Confessions of an Actor*. London: Routledge.

Wills, G and Cooper, CL (1988) *Pressure Sensitive: Popular Musicians Under Stress*. London: Sage.

Fame

COPING WITH FAME

"Fame and tranquillity can never be bedfellows." Montaigne

The stresses of fame are many. Once people have tasted success, how do they deal with failure? How do they deal with those episodes of stage fright that often accompany being in the public eye? How do they respond to stress? How do they cope with and recover from burnout and mental exhaustion? How do they cope with growing old – do they carry on regardless, make comebacks or start a second career? Fame may sometimes be a brief candle, or the 'tinsel' that falls from above and then is gone, but famous people still have real lives to live out.

The subject matter of motivation, coping with stress, performance anxiety, burnout and careers advice is one that occurs regularly in any sport psychology centre or specialist arts and media therapy practice. Much of the material below is taken from experience in dealing with well-known clients at the London based Arts Psychology Consultants. It includes data on, for example, dancers who use the service for careers advice during transition and resettlement, and actors and musicians seeking strategies to deal with performance anxiety, burnout or career issues.

Famous people have the same basic human needs and problems as others. The main difference is that they live in the limelight, often under great pressure, and when the going gets tough many have vivid fantasies about simply dropping out or escaping. Some do escape, like actor Stephen Fry, or disappear mysteriously like Ritchie Edwards of the Manic Street Preachers. Others take time off, frequently through exhaustion. However, the overwhelming majority carry on, because their careers are more important than fame itself, and the desire to improve and exercise their talent is fundamental to them.

FAILING SAFE – THE KEY TO SUCCEEDING
"If a thing's worth doing, it is worth doing badly." GK Chesterton

Everything in our lives is vulnerable to failure – equipment, plans, careers, marriages. People's bodies give out, even rocks wear out. Everything has some kind of 'sell by date'. Yet fame exists within a 'success' culture. Famous people have made it to the top. If you judge success as a journey from the bottom up everything gets better – more work, more income, more acclaim. If you judge everything from the top down, however, then the concept of failure can seem catastrophic. The reality, however, is that careers are full of ups and downs, as expressed by actor Paul Clemens: "It's so difficult for a young actor in Hollywood today – you're on your own. When you go up for a role you're either too young, too fat or too thin, unless somebody already has you in mind. Just getting the interviews for roles is tough – as is making sure that the agent doesn't lose sight of you. Frustration is your constant companion in Hollywood, but when things all come together as they did for me in 'A Death in Canaan' you know why you've chosen the profession. After Canaan, which was such a success, I accepted the first feature film offer that came along. It died." (May 1984, in McClelland, 1985).

Fear of failure can be acute in well-known sportspeople, as Dr Adrian Taylor notes: "Fear of failure has been identified as a leading source of stress among many involved in sport, particularly among the younger age groups and those at elite levels. Those who tend to place winning very highly, or who have committed most to succeeding and are also less confident of their own ability, are likely to be the ones who fear failure the most." (Bull, 1991)

So how do people manage failure? When learning to sail a dinghy they practise capsizing and righting it, in judo they learn to fall, when they occupy a new building they practise the fire drill. Situations are manageable – even predictable – when one knows the routine for dealing with failure. They are nerve-racking or even dangerous when one doesn't. One danger is to build expectations on an exaggerated degree of hope. Hope contains the wish that good things will happen. It's other pole, disappointment, is the realisation that bad things can happen, have happened and will happen. If life is built on hope rather than a healthy objective sense of reality, disappointment can catapult a person into depression, despair and a feeling of being let down or even 'heartbroken'.

Relying on a continual cycle of hope and disappointment is therefore a naïve strategy for approaching success. It is much better to adopt a long-term strategy which allows for failure at any or every stage, but does not exclude later success – athlete Linford Christie notably won the Olympic 100m in his thirties. Steady progress towards this sort of excellence is achieved through a positive attitude to setbacks – setbacks become learning events, and as crucial to doing well as success itself. What is ideally required is a steady increase in potential, not a roller coaster ride of hope and despair. Important factors are attitude, bravery, belief in the power of hard work, positive response to threat, achievable goal setting, flexibility and constant re-assessment of the situation. As they say in the world of opera, 'it's not over until the fat lady sings'.

Also essential when handling a setback is the ability to put it into perspective. A career setback like a bad appearance, show or film, or a book project being turned down, is not a catastrophe – it cannot be compared to a real catastrophe such as an earthquake or a war. It also requires the ability to focus carefully on the incident in question ('Thursday was a bad night') rather than 'globalising' setbacks ('I'll never ever be able to walk onto a stage anywhere again').

When setbacks do happen, it is important to learn to recover quick-ly, otherwise chronic stress can turn into depression. Studies with nurses in Accident and Emergency units show that recovery rates from traumatic experiences vary greatly between individuals. Those who suffer most long term stress are those who take weeks or more to recover from bad experiences, which linger in the mind and disturb sleep. Those who suffer the least stress are those who can mentally and emotionally deal with problems within a few days, after which recovery is quite rapid. When thrown by a horse, as the saying goes, get straight back on it again.

Like wrong notes played by accident when improvising, failure can lead people into unexpected and even more constructive directions. Such was the case with magician Tommy Cooper's debut at the age of 17. "Intending to give a serious display of magic, He walked on to the stage. As soon as the curtains parted, he forgot all his lines. Everything went wrong. His grand finale was the milk bottle trick. 'You have a bottle full of milk and you put paper over the top. You turn the bottle upside down and take the paper away', he told the entranced audi-ence. He took away the paper. Drenched. All over him. He then got stage fright and began working his mouth furiously without any sound coming out. At this point he started to tremble and walked off, perspir-ing heavily. Once in the wings, he heard the massed cheers of a standing ovation. His future glory was assured." (Pile, 1980)

It is unfortunate that in our success culture parents may tell their children that failure is unacceptable. While rewarding and cultivating cleverness and achievement, they pass on no knowledge about how to deal with setbacks or failures, setting them up for a later fall. There are a number of well-known people who have, as actors say, 'been lucky' and have only had to deal with failure in later stages of their career. The capacity to see failures in scale, to accept them and then go forward to greater things (as politician and writer Jeffrey Archer did when facing acute financial problems early in his career) is one of the key qualities of winners, whether in performing, in sport or in life.

PERFORMANCE ANXIETY, AND HOW TO DEAL WITH IT

It is difficult to be in the public eye without having to face large numbers of people – live audiences, radio and television audiences, chat shows and personal appearances requiring speeches. Performers, who face audiences nightly, call stage fright 'the pearlies' or 'the shakes', and at some stage in their careers more than half of them have some experience of attacks. 'Performance Anxiety' is the term used to cover general aspects of this affliction, since it can happen in many other locations besides stages. Athletes get it at the trackside, snooker players at the snooker table, politicians before important speeches, businessmen before giving presentations. Famous people are particularly prone since they also feel they have to keep up high standards befitting their image.

More accurately, they have experienced the 'adrenaline response' when appearing in front of the public. This 'alert' mechanism derives from our biological ancestors who had to decide between fight or flight when facing danger. An alert body state will make the heart beat faster to send more blood round the system, tense the major muscles ready for action, sweat to lose heat when running, and inhibit digestion so blood goes to the muscles where it is needed. Sensible for cavemen, maybe, but fairly uncomfortable for performing precise mental and physical tasks in front of others! The combination gives sufferers the familiar thumping heart, swimming head and queasy feeling that affects them just before they have to face an audience.

Surveys show this adrenaline response is common to all people who face audiences, and highest in the five or ten minutes preceding and following the moment of going on stage. So why, then, in a survey by pharmacologist Dr Ian James, did 60% of orchestral musicians consider 'nerves' detrimental to performance, 9% feel they made no difference and 15% think they actually improved performance? The answer lies not in the body, but in the belief. Those of us who tend to panic, and who have previous experience of performing badly, may believe they are caught up in a repetitive cycle. The toughened professionals think that a few minutes of extra-alertness is par for the course. The courageous may, like boxers or racing drivers, get a kick out of confrontation. Broadcasting staff often prefer to transmit live because of the extra 'tingle', which they call 'red light fever'. It is the interpretation, the 'emotional labelling' and the ability to handle the situation that makes the difference. The adrenaline is the same.

The usual mental worries are those of being judged, as in sporting events, speeches, competitions, or auditions, and this may be worse when the event takes place in front of a 'learned' audience, or when it is being recorded or filmed. One famous rock musician (who had played live in front of millions) experienced the worst nerves of his career in a TV broadcast where he had to play in front of a legendary childhood hero on the same instrument. The anxiety often precedes the performance itself, either when rehearsing or simply at home building up a state of dread. Performance anxiety is associated with diverse situations of being 'listened to', 'looked at', 'judged' or 'criticised'. And such criticism is not only external – self induced criticism can be even more debilitating. Popular musicians in a survey conducted through the Musicians' Union stated that their highest stress factor was "feeling you must reach or maintain the standards of musicianship you set for yourself." (Wills and Cooper, 1988)

THE MYTHS ABOUT STAGE FRIGHT

Part of the reason that performance anxiety remains such a scourge to people in the limelight is the mythology that tends to surround it. Examples of this are:

Myth: "If your heart is beating fast and you have the shakes you have stage fright."

Rapid heartbeat, shakes and other symptoms are produced by adrenaline. However, such bodily effects are equally associated with emotions other than fear. A person would experience similar bodily symptoms when aggressively aroused (before a boxing match), when happily aroused (during a sexual orgasm) or when simply physically aroused and feeling no emotion at all (when working out in the gym).

Fame

It is crucial to break this automatic association between the adrenaline that is affecting the body and the emotion of fear, so that the emotional response becomes either neutral or positive.

Myth: "There are 'good nerves' and 'bad nerves' – 'good nerves' can work in your favour."

The expression 'nerves' is ambiguous and unhelpful. In one sense it describes the physical effects of adrenaline (a nervous physical state). In another sense it describes the emotion of fear (feeling nervous). As stated, it is crucial to break this association between adrenaline and fear, and the word 'nerves' itself can cement these together. What 'good nerves' usually means is an alert body state and a positive emotional buzz or challenge. The expression sounds like a contradiction in terms, however, and should not imply that 'fear is good'. There is a popular self-help book entitled 'Feel the Fear and Do It Anyway' (Jeffers, 1992). A better definition, in terms of defeating stage fright, would be Feel the Adrenaline and Do It Anyway.

Myth: "You need to feel nervous at the start of a performance otherwise it's no good."

There is a lot of sense in this idea, although it may sound like nonsense. Once again, 'nervous' should not be thought to mean 'fearful'. You can then say 'If you feel physically over-aroused at the start of performance (as nearly all performers do) then after ten minutes or so you will settle back into your optimum state of performance arousal and the performance should go fine. But if you are under-aroused even at the start, through tiredness or whatever, you may not be alert enough to give of your best.' The optimum level of performance judged by others tends to occur at a point where the performer may subjectively feel over-aroused (Wilson, 1997), which further explains this myth and may help to reassure the performer that arousal is not as detrimental as may be imagined.

Myths like the above have been around for a long time, because in many ways performance anxiety is badly understood and performers are unnecessarily resigned to suffering in silence from it. There are now good cognitive techniques and strategies to analyse and deal with the problem, and sufferers can be helped to reduce the level of panic to quite manageable proportions. Predisposing factors can be many and varied and go back to one's earliest years, and different things trigger anxiety in different people. It may be mainly situational - being on stage or in front of people. It may be interpersonal – being oversensitive to the criticisms and expectations of other people. It may be motivational – allowing inner doubts to affect performance. It may be associated with the body not doing what it is supposed to either through bad technique, pain or posture problems. It may be associated with the long-term effects of burnout. The commonly encountered forms of performance anxiety are the following – note that one or several can be present.

STAGE FRIGHT AS A LEARNED RESPONSE
This, the classic form of stage fright, is where previous bad performing experiences condition us to expect 'catastrophes' to happen. This melodramatic sense of disaster is typically disproportionate to what is really happening (eg 'I'll be sick over everyone, run off stage as everyone laughs at me and never work again'). It originates in various mishaps as diverse as school performances, early stage performances and Such mishaps weld together fear and performing, as Russian experimental psychologist Pavlov's dogs, when presented with food and the ring of a bell at the same time, came to associate a bell with salivating. The ever lurking threat thereafter is that 'if it can happen once, it can happen again'. untypically bad nights.

Essential in dealing with this is to confront the melodrama as irrational. Examined in detail, such initial 'establishing' mishaps are freak combinations of a cluster of circumstances that are most unlikely to re-occur (feeling sick, arriving late, instruments not working, difficult directors, things going wrong on the set, for instance). The anxiety is also controllable, as proved by the fact that actors, musicians and sportspeople routinely perform through it. Rarely if ever does it result in a catastrophe. A sense of scale here is vital – catastrophes are things like wars and plagues. Missed cues and memory lapses are survivable, and need not ruin careers. Likewise, nerves are only nerves – they do not need to develop into panic if one avoids being melodramatic. Body control also helps: when nervous, breathe out slowly and deliberately, and drop the shoulders to relax the neck.

FEAR OF FELLOW PERFORMERS
Fame can be a bitchy environment, and a further typical form of stage fright is fear of criticism from one's fellows in the performing, political

or sport environment. It is not unknown for well-known people to have nightmares about those they work with or to walk off stages or sets in disgust. Criticism of the self and others is in the nature of the performing beast, but careless criticism can reinforce previously stored 'curses' from parents, teachers or critics, like 'you'll never make it to the top' or 'you're too nervous to perform'. The antidote to criticism is to cultivate a spirit of generosity – to be kind to others and, most importantly, to oneself. When confronted by people with attitude, it is helpful to remember that their emotional junk is their problem. The 'fundamental attribution error' in psychology is in attributing 'bad things' to oneself. Because it is so fundamental – since childhood we worry that we have done something wrong when parents are angry or there is a bad mood in the room – it is worth taking steps to correct this. It is no accident that the term includes the word 'error', so if there is a personality clash, examine the external reasons before the internal ones – a person's anger may be due to circumstances like tax demands, cars getting parking tickets and so on.

FEAR OF ONE'S SELF

We all have two secret fantasies: that we are 'really marvellous' and that we are 'really not that good at all'. Well-known people are just as prone to this as any other middle ranking sportsperson or performer. How can two such irreconcilable fantasies co-exist? In an effort to reconcile this paradox people can delude themselves in a variety of clever ways:

* By never putting their talent fully to the test, not auditioning, developing strange physical pains or giving up entirely.

* By making some excuse for not being 100% on form, like being drunk or always arriving late.

* By becoming rebels that 'nobody really understands'.

* By secretly believing they are a fraud, and suffering constant anxiety that one day their shortcomings will be discovered.

In the face of such self-doubt, it is particularly important to acquire a belief in 'The Constant Self' (Evans, 1994). This is doubly important because one of the persistent underlying fears of stage fright is the worry that it is unpredictable. Its random nature eats away particularly at those who like to plan their lives. Everyone in the entertainment world understands the ups and downs of the profession, but many of the factors that cause these are external. The audience, director, venue and acoustics vary from one night to another. Physical and emotional state varies. Relationships vary. Schedules vary – there are days of 4 hours sleep or 12 hours work or both. But ability in general is pretty constant, although it may not always be perceived as such. The important ways to stabilise expectations are:

* Constant practice, to maintain predictably high levels of performance. This is basic to sport and dance, but should not be ignored in any high profile profession.

* Shifting awareness away from distracting inner dialogue and onto the performance and fellow performers when on stage or competing in sport. This is the basis of the 'Inner Game' books.

* Believing that basic talent and ability is constant. People are not 'only as good as their last performance'. This oft-touted myth is harmful nonsense – people are as good as the talent they have nurtured and practised year in, year out. Far too many people judge themselves solely by odd mistakes they make or bad nights. In reality this is a tiny percentage compared with the total effect of a life's talent and professionalism.

Those who take determined steps to conquer stage fright usually find they make good progress. Their goal is to replace melodramatic fears of catastrophe with controllable nerves. Typically this is achieved in a sort of saw-tooth progress, with better and worse days but a steady overall improvement. With this improvement comes the replacement of a negative self-image – 'I'm a person who suffers a lot from stage fright' – with a positive one – 'I get a few nerves like everyone else, but it rarely stops me performing as usual, so I don't worry too much about it'.

A full account of dealing with stage fright in musicians is found in 'The Secrets of Musical Confidence' (Evans, 1994).

BURNOUT
Burnout is a word coined in the mid 1970s, and its use as a description for 'physical, emotional, spiritual, intellectual and interpersonal exhaustion' became popular in the 80s as a byproduct of contemporary research into job stress. Though the focus of such research was the corporate world, clearly high job stress, personal frustration and inadequate coping skills are just as likely to affect well known people

Fame

of all kinds, and certainly performing artists. A clear indication of this is seen in Wills and Cooper (1988) which documents the stressors experienced by popular musicians, and was founded on a questionnaire circulated to British Musician's Union members.

Burnout is something that sport psychologists also deal with regularly, and may be both psychological and physical: "Athletes may experience psychological burnout when under intense pressure for some time. There is a progressive loss of idealism, energy and purpose. The loss of physical and emotional energy may also be accompanied by negative attitudes and the belief that less is being accomplished. In later stages of burnout there is commonly a decline in interest to the point where complete withdrawal or dropout takes place. Athletes become repelled by an activity which once provided a deep source of personal satisfaction." (Dr. Adrian Taylor, in Bull, 1991).

The typical age when burnout occurs is generally assumed to be between the ages of 30 to 45; the 'mid life crisis' where the importance and satisfaction of many factors in life are re-evaluated. It can also occur in the late forties, where the feeling may stem more from the notion of 'can I still manage?' Some stars make compromises or lighten their schedules at the start of artistic decline. Burnout can, however, occur earlier for various reasons. The first is in child actors and child prodigies, who may have been appearing in public for 15 years by the time they turn 21, and this also applies to sportspeople who have started training very young. Brilliant snooker player Ronnie O'Sullivan is only one example of how motivation problems can occur in the early twenties. Performing artists are appearing at a younger age on TV, in popular music and even in classical music – forming the backbone of the media's youth culture. As a result, teenage stars may not be far behind in burnout potential.

Burnout also occurs as a result of sheer pressure spread over a few hectic years. The huge size and budgets of modern media companies and their world-wide coverage mean that stars are hyped very quickly to global celebrity status, and then required to meet the pressure with gruelling schedules that make them 'good value for money'. This can be worse still in the case of prize winners of international competitions, where there is added pressure to surpass one's peers. The substitution of studio-based bands for touring bands may also mean that newly created stars may simply not have the psychological readiness or strength of experience to cope. In general our contemporary 'pressure to succeed' culture is forcing young people into pushing themselves harder in an increasingly competitive mental environment where league tables and award ceremonies are everyday phenomena.

Burnout can result from either underwork career stress or overwork career stress. In actors, because of the constant periods of resting between engagements, the problem is chronic underwork stress. This leads to worries about one's self worth and melodramatic images of never working again, allied to feelings of passiveness, futility and having to rely entirely on agents and casting directors to get work. Whilst one would assume that famous actors have a reasonably steady stream of work, periods of unemployment characterise the profession from top to bottom.

In musicians it is usually the opposite – overwork stress from schedules most people would consider ridiculous: up at 7.30am, travelling in the morning, afternoon rehearsal, sound check in the late afternoon then evening concert and not in bed before midnight. That may be a good day – some tour schedules are worse still, and we haven't yet mentioned recording sessions.

LOST PASSION AND CAREER SETBACKS

Most performers and sportspeople start their love affair with their chosen activity – often at an early age – with somewhere near 100% passion and 0% knowledge and disillusionment with the profession. Over a period of years, passion goes down and disillusionment rises to the critical mass of 51% disillusionment, 49% passion. After that the enjoyment of the performing life goes into negative equity and progressive burnout ensues. Performing becomes more disagreeable than agreeable. This is 'spiritual and emotional burnout'. (Evans, 1997, proceedings of York International Conference 'Health and the Musician'.) Without knowing it, one hits a career plateau where the typical work schedule is fairly similar day in day out, and this applies equally to famous artists as to rank and file performers. Composer and conductor Pierre Boulez is said to have remarked to a violinist he was conducting: "You are more fortunate than me – my career is the same every year, but once you were an orchestral player and now you are a soloist. Your career is going up."

Fame

Youthful energy steadily burns out, revealing any number of underlying tensions from disillusion with the profession to concern about the future. Ambition gives place to apathy as careers become more predictable and less varied and challenging. Where there is chronic performance anxiety, as with some stars, there may be a feeling of 'I can't stand it any more – either I reduce the anxiety or I'm giving my career up just to keep me sane'. Loss of motivation may have caused a fall in professional standards – sometimes falling to the minimum acceptable level – which may have been noticed by others before it really hits the person concerned. There may be a sudden awareness that denial is no longer an adequate defence – one is only just coping. This sudden peak in anxiety may be dramatically worse in famous performers who have heavy advance bookings, sometimes stretching ahead for months and years. Fear may turn into alarm as the performer fights against a constant desire to call for help. Getting permission from a doctor to have a break or admitting oneself to a health clinic is a common outcome.

Burnout can be a reaction to one major career disappointment or 'heartbreak', or to an accumulation of medium setbacks. Setbacks can be worse with creative types, who put a lot of their personal ideas into projects, and the let down may be more personally received. They can be accompanied by the feeling of being betrayed by others in the business, or of having been cheated financially by agent, manager or media company. There is a paradoxical effect where the worst setbacks can happen when one is closest to the highest goal. As hopes are raised towards the mental acceptance of achieving fame, setbacks can burst the whole narcissistic bubble, with a huge let down and sudden depression, anger and feelings of hopelessness, which can trigger years off work.

SYMPTOMS AND REMEDIES FOR BURNOUT

Common symptoms of apathetic burnout in performers include not practising or rehearsing enough, not warming up before performances and arriving late for rehearsals or minutes before performance. Performing itself may contain mistakes or memory slips, and performers may not listen attentively enough to others around them, simply concentrating on getting their own part right. There may be heavy drug or alcohol use (sometimes initiated 'to counteract nerves' but then continued to excess) which camouflages the burnout and can easily be taken at first glance by medical and other practitioners to be the main thing wrong. There is often guilt at falling technical standards, dread of the future or chronic depression. Burnout may mirror apathy in other areas (marriage, sex, lapsed hobbies, lapsed sport due to over-weight). There may be several common depressive features, such as a sense of 'not looking backwards to ones birth but onwards towards death' – fantasies one wanted to accomplish in one's lifetime may no longer be possible, particularly in career terms. Burned out people may be temperamental and snappy when challenged about their condi-tion, since they may be in various stages of denial. When allowed to see their problem as burnout, however, most people are quick to recog-nise symptoms, willing to talk about it, and with guidance can usually make some key career changes that will improve the situation.

Even for the famous, life on the mid-life plateau can be successfully managed so as to give variety and enjoyment. This may not be the hectic all-consuming buzz of ambitious youth following the first big break, but it is much better than apathy and loss of passion. There is a revival of interest and commitment, and a replacement of disillusion-ment with values such as pleasure, creativity, variety and learning new things – all key job values in performers (Evans, 1994). New priorities are holidays, sleep, pacing work, making periods of calm around impor-tant shows, getting help with children or household tasks if needed, and simply learning to say no so that schedules are not overwhelming. Freshness is imperative to one's career, so there is a need to positively recharge in time out – not just vegetate or do boring tasks. When asked after a TV masterclass whether he was going on to Paris to work, top jazz bassist Ray Brown replied in astonishment "I go to Paris to eat!".

Exercise and physical fitness are important, particularly for tours which take one into overdrive – Irish band U2 have stated they could not cope with touring without a regime of work outs in the gym. Also important are outside interests, hobbies and quality time with friends. If stage fright is a problem, effective counselling should be considered. To bring some of the old passion back, it can be fun to do shows with friends or charity events – in other words to perform for pleasure. There is a long history of classical musicians playing chamber music with friends, as in the magical concerts led by Heifetz, Casals and Menuhin.

Fame

TO WORK OR NOT TO WORK – AGEING IN THE PROFESSION OR GIVING IT UP

"You can't retire in Hollywood. Nobody gives up a job, even if he's ninety or sick or has money like Midas... Everybody works until the last breath." Lionel Barrymore (McClelland, 1985)

There are many examples of stars that worked well on into old age – Lillian Gish, George Burns, Bob Hope, John Gielgud, Anthony Quinn, Olivia de Havilland, Katharine Hepburn. Sylvia Sidney appeared in the Fantasy Island series at 88, and Dame Judith Anderson was in 'Santa Barbara' until shortly before death aged 94. TV soaps, in fact, are refuges for many of the screen stars like Joan Bennett, Ann Sheridan and Dorothy Malone, some like Joan Crawford and Elizabeth Taylor simply making guest appearances. Getting older can give rise to a number of potential stress factors: having to defend one's position against a hungry new generation, dealing with natural physical decline including some inevitable fall-off in reasoning ability, memory problems in learning new material, and the almost equally inevitable aches and pains (including tinnitus in musicians). It means keeping fresh and avoiding burnout, boredom and becoming disillusioned with the business.

Some people, however, do give up earlier. The key reason for giving up in one's thirties is loss of peak bodily function. This is typically the age when sportspeople and ballet dancers give up. The body starts to work a little less well than before, then conspicuously less well. Work starts to thin out, then dry up completely. The answer to this may be – like boxers – to quit while on top. Ballet dancers in the major companies in the UK, and also in other countries like Canada, have a good system of dealing with what they call 'transition'. They contribute into a fund over a 10 year period while dancing, after which they can take out several thousands to pay for college education, retraining and essential hardware like computers.

COMEBACKS

Some stars who give up are persuaded back into the profession by good offers. Others simply lurk around ready to make comebacks. Whilst for dancers and sportspeople this is unlikely, musicians and actors – like writers and artists – have no particular physical handicaps with age. Sinatra's comebacks continued for years, and pianists such as Horowitz returned several times after periods off the concert platform. While some comebacks are as contrived as a series of concert encores, others are quite genuine, and enable stars who still enjoy their work to earn good money, feel young again and relive some of the old adrenaline and excitement. Performing may simply continue to be what they do best in life. Some, like Veronica Lake and James Dunn, went bankrupt and were forced into comebacks. Others found new artistic directions, as Paul Simon did with Graceland.

The public seems to have no difficulty in sympathising with the ageing process in sports like snooker and golf (Steve Davis and Mark O'Meara winning major championships in their forties), because this fits the age profile that these sports enjoy within the general public. The difficulty comes with activities that have a younger population profile, such as football, boxing, rock music or romantic lead roles. The comeback may be acceptable to the public if the person in question 'comes back' in different roles and with an appropriately older image. Well loved stars like Don Ameche, who was popular in the 30s and 40s and re-appeared in the 80s with 'Trading Places' ('83) and 'Cocoon '('85), proved that 'old age' comebacks are not only viable but well accepted. One of the most tragic attempts at a return to the limelight was that of boxer Joe Louis, who took a beating in the ring in an attempt to earn money to pay off his tax debts.

Middle age comebacks often happen to stars who would say they had never really been away, like Elvis or Tina Turner. John Travolta and Richard Gere were two stars that had periods when their fame dipped, though they continued working. When they happened to get into the right films ('Pulp Fiction' and 'Pretty Woman') they then made well publicised returns to the A list. Others played the comeback for laughs, as Victor Mature did in Neil Simon's 'After the Fox' and Leslie Nielson did to even greater success in 'Airplane' and the 'Naked Gun' films.

But in some cases public opinion is divided. How many 'comeback tours' can bands like The Rolling Stones do and still remain credible? Financially they remain very credible – nostalgia can sell out tickets, as their mid nineties tours, like those of Herman and the Hermits and the Troggs, proved. But psychologically there starts to enter into the equation a note of discord. Are comebacks eventually sad? To carry on trying to be active and youthful as we age is the true human condition – so performers who do this are surely only 'sad' if we think getting old is sad. In many cases this is exactly what we do feel, because age is a sensitive taboo and because we like to believe in the fantasy that our stars are eternally young, rather than seeing in them the wrinkles that remind us too closely of our own mortality. When stars like Brigitte Bardot age realistically they even attract anger that they have not tried to prolong the make-believe with plastic surgery, that they have not colluded with our own states of denial.

SECOND CAREERS

It is better to have a 'plan B' for dealing with life after fame, rather than stumbling into it. Good examples of second careers are buying and dealing in property, investing wisely, opening an interesting company, going into production, writing a book, becoming a chat-show host, or that other essential career of starting a family. The most emotionally and often financially fulfilled of the ex-stars are often the ones with new careers or families to occupy them. The effectiveness of second careers – and the benefit of starting them sooner rather than later – should not be underestimated. Some are major achievements in their own right, while many have brought in more money than the original path to fame.

Ronald Reagan put politics firmly on the map as a second career, becoming 40th president of the US. Other famous national leaders were pianist Ignace Paderewski and writer Vaclav Havel. Ambassadors have included Sidney Poitier (Bermudan Ambassador to Japan) and Shirley Temple (US Ambassador to Ghana, then Czechoslovakia). Mayors include Clint Eastwood (Carmel) and Sonny Bono (Palm Springs). Fred Dalton Thompson is a US Senator, and Glenda Jackson is Minister of Transport in the British Labour Government.

TV is a common second career after films. In fact, more money can be made in chat shows than in the movies. Loretta Young retired from films in 1953 and began a second, equally successful career with 'The Loretta Young Show,' a half-hour drama anthology series which ran on NBC-TV from September 1953 to September 1961, picking up Emmy Awards in 1954, 1956 and 1958. Oprah Winfrey, who had already worked as a news anchor for WJZ Television in Baltimore in the late 1970s, was listed as one of twelve "Promising New Actors of 1985" in John Willis' Screen World, Vol 37. Her real fame, however, started the following year with the Oprah Winfrey Show.

REAL ESTATE, INVESTMENTS AND NEW BUSINESSES
Owning and controlling one's own material is one way of going into business. Oprah Winfrey is only one of many stars who made the astute decision to buy into their own shows and rights. Harold Lloyd owned all his films, as did William Boyd (Hopalong Cassidy), who sold his ranch to buy his rights and made a fortune out of Saturday morning shows. United Artists was a co-operative founded by the stars themselves. Rights are huge business these days, and are even exchanged between stars – Michael Jackson currently owns The Beatles rights, a process they themselves started with the creation of Apple. For people who work in the media industry and know it well, it may be a good place to channel financial investment.

Investing in real estate is a favourite with the stars. Dana Andrews retired from films in the Sixties and made, he said, more money from real estate than he ever did in movies. Bob Hope invested his money in real estate in Los Angeles which made him vastly wealth. However, when he was interviewed in the 80s he claimed his wealth was nothing like that of Fred MacMurray – who bought most of the San Fernando Valley for chum change and was at one time the world's richest (ex) actor. Gene Autry retired from acting and bought hotels, real estate, radio stations, the California Angels baseball team and as fellow actors joked "half of Southern California". Randolph Scott made several hundred million dollars as a result of superb investments, and spent his remaining years avoiding film industry affairs and playing golf with a whole raft of other showbiz figures.

Business ventures as second careers have been many and varied. Restaurant owners include Jack Dempsey, The Rolling Stones, Kelly McGillis, Arnold Schwarzenegger, Sylvester Stallone, Tom Selleck, Christy Turlington, Michael Caine and Terence Conran, while Jane Asher sells food products under her own name. Francis Ford Coppola owns and operates a California vineyard making Rubicon wine, while Brian Donlevy is into mining gold and tungsten. Dolly Parton has her own theme park "Dollywood", William Holden became co-owner of the Mount Kenya Safari Club. Quentin Tarrantino and Madonna own record companies. Racehorse breeding was the sideline of Audie Murphy and Bing Crosby, who like Bob Hope, Helen Traubel and Gene Autry also

Fame

had major interests in baseball teams.

Women have used their physique and beauty to found Health and Beauty businesses. In the 80s Jane Fonda started the aerobic exercise craze with the publication of 'The Jane Fonda Workout Book'. Other health gurus include Goldie Hawn and Linda Evans, who owns fitness centres in 15 locations. Elizabeth Taylor has a range of perfume products named after gemstones.

If all else fails there is always the autobiography.

REFERENCES

Bull, Stephen J (1991) *Sport Psychology*, Marlborough Wilts. UK, The Crowood Press

Evans, Andrew (1994) *The Secrets of Musical Confidence*, London, HarperCollins

Jeffers, Susan (1992) *Feel the Fear and Do It Anyway*, Fawcett

McClelland, Doug (1985) *Hollywood on Hollywood – Tinsel Town Talks* Winchester MA USA:

Pile, Stephen (1980) *The Book of Heroic Failures*, London, Book Club Associates

Wills, G and Cooper, CL (1988) *Pressure Sensitive: Popular Musicians Under Stress*. London: Sage.

Wilson, GD (1997) *Performance Anxiety*, In Hargreaves DJ and North AC (eds.) *The Social Psychology of Music*, NY Oxford University Press.

The International Movie Database: www.imdb.com

Arts Psychology Consultants:

www.artspsychology.mcmail.com.

Tel: 0207 602 2707

INDEX

Fame

Fame

Fame